1 & 2
Timothy

I0142322

GARY R. SMALL

1 & 2 Timothy
Copyright © 2024 by Gary R. Small

Print ISBN: 978-1-4866-2528-4
eBook ISBN: 978-1-4866-2529-1

Word Alive Press
119 De Baets Street, Winnipeg, MB R2J 3R9
www.wordalivepress.ca

WORD ALIVE
—**P R E S S**—

Cataloguing in Publication may be obtained through Library and Archives Canada

Contents

Series Introduction	v
Foreword	ix
Introduction: 1 Timothy	xi
1. Command: 1 Timothy 1:1–2	1
2. Pure Heart: 1 Timothy 1:3–7	4
3. Glorious Gospel: 1 Timothy 1:8–11	9
4. Given Strength: 1 Timothy 1:12–17	12
5. Holding On to Faith: 1 Timothy 1:18–20	17
6. Intercession: 1 Timothy 2:1–7	21
7. Modestly: 1 Timothy 2:8–15	25
8. Aspire: 1 Timothy 3:1–7	32
9. Service: 1 Timothy 3:8–13	37
10. Sing: 1 Timothy 3:14–16	40
11. Extraordinary Godliness: 1 Timothy 4:1–10	43
12. Persevere: 1 Timothy 4:11–16	47
13. Prescribe: 1 Timothy 5:1–8	51
14. Help: 1 Timothy 5:9–16	55

15. Keep Pure: 1 Timothy 5:17–25   59

16. Great Gain: 1 Timothy 6:1–10   63

17. Take Hold: 1 Timothy 6:11–21   68

18. Reflections: 1 Timothy   73

19. Introduction: 2 Timothy   77

20. Identity: 2 Timothy 1:1–2   81

21. Self-Discipline: 2 Timothy 1:3–10   85

22. Know: 2 Timothy 1:11–18   90

23. Reflect: 2 Timothy 2:1–13   96

24. Instruments: 2 Timothy 2:14–26   101

25. Godliness: 2 Timothy 3:1–9   106

26. Convinced: 2 Timothy 3:10–17   110

27. The Word: 2 Timothy 4:1–5   115

28. Crown of Righteousness: 2 Timothy 4:6–8   120

29. Stand By: 2 Timothy 4:9–21   126

30. Your Spirit: 2 Timothy 4:22   130

    Reflections: 2 Timothy   133

    For Further Reading   137

Series Introduction

Keep this Book of the Law always on your lips; meditate on it day and night, so that you may be careful to do everything written in it. Then you will be prosperous and successful. (Joshua 1:8)

The word meditate and its derivatives occur eighteen times in the Bible. Of these, eight pertain to meditating on the Scriptures. Through these verses, we are encouraged to hold God's word in our hearts so that we might profit from His wisdom and be blessed by a closer relationship with Him (Psalm 119:1–3).

The secular world has also proposed the concept of taking a thoughtful approach to life and uses the word mindfulness to describe a thoughtful, meditative approach to life.

Mindfulness has been defined as "the awareness that arises through paying attention in the present moment, on purpose, nonjudgmentally."[1] Other terms have been applied to this intentional approach, such as *to internalize*, *to meditate on*, or *to process*. It is what we as Christians do when we carefully consider the Bible.

---

1 Judson Brewer, *Unwinding Anxiety* (New York, NY: Avery, 2021), 71. Quoting Jon Kabat-Zinn.

The trouble is that we often don't have time to study in this manner. Instead we find ourselves snatching moments in our busy lives to read, internalize, and digest passages from our daily reading of the Bible. By squeezing these most important moments of the day into the least number of minutes, we don't make time for the mindfulness required to truly digest God's word.

Another mistake we often fall into is having too high expectations of ourselves. We lean into weighty commentaries or topical novels on life-changing subjects and once again find that we don't have the sufficient time or headspace to do justice to the meaty subjects therein.

We previously referred to this problem as having too much pace and not sufficient peace to make sense of God's word. It is the challenge that led to the production of this series of books, which are designed to help lift a word from His word and make it poignant.

How we choose to use the selected word for each chapter will be different for each reader. Each chapter is designed to provoke mindful thought on a biblical passage. We have also provided three applications at the end of each chapter to stimulate further reflection.

It is hoped that the chosen word from each passage will be recalled throughout the day when we find moments of stillness or thought, so we can pay attention, on purpose, nonjudgmentally.

These books can be used by individuals. They may also find use in group settings to provoke further discussion on a sermon series or in small group Bible study.

It is hoped that the books will be used as a spiritual tool to reinvigorate your Bible reading and provide impetus to make a life change as a Christian.

The concept is simple, one which by no means seeks to detract from the value of in-depth Bible study. There is still a place for this when time allows and further reading references are provided. We have taken care to tread a middle road theologically and avoid weighty arguments on some finer points of hermeneutics, although some of these can be found within the referenced material.

We sincerely hope that *A Word from His Word* will not only lift selected words from the pages of Scripture but also provide a lift to your Bible reading and spiritual life.

Much has been made by the secular world of the benefits of mindfulness. I suspect this discipline is not new, although it has perhaps been lost in our striving for scientific purpose. Yet there is, in this series, an opportunity to rediscover the usefulness of intentional meditation on God's word (Psalm 1:1–2).

Foreword

I have known Gary for well over a decade and have had the pleasure of teaching his children at St Timothy's, at St Paul University, and at the University of Ottawa. I was pleased when he asked me to write this foreword to his devotional work on the letters to Timothy, and not only because the school where I teach is the namesake of the letter's recipient.

Gary's approach to the letters is humble, generous to the reader (and to his author), but not dogmatic, and he likes to open broad avenues for exploration in his explication of the letters. In doing so, he avoids some of the more contentious issues surrounding the letters (e.g. the identity of the author and his attitude towards women) and helps to focus on what is helpful to us—the author's caring and practical approach to Christian life.

In this way, Gary's work conveys a warm sense of permanence, of the value of Bible study in what seems to us an increasingly fractious world.

Gary's reflection on Timothy 4:16 is typical of his generous approach and is something that I have tried to convey to my students: "we read our Bibles so we can better understand Him and align ourselves accordingly. In understanding Him, we come to know ourselves better. In the process, we acknowledge where we have work to do."

—Dr. Michael Klaassen
St. Timothy's Classical Academy, Ottawa

Introduction

1 TIMOTHY

In 1 and 2 Timothy, Paul wrote to one of his closest disciples. Both letters are different in context and in their content, and both have different aims. 1 Timothy was written by Paul around AD 63 probably from Philippi in Macedonia while he was a free-man.

Before we begin studying 1 Timothy, it is useful to consider the relationship between these close friends. If we tune in to the temperaments, traits, and mindsets, we will be better positioned to understand why Paul wrote and how Timothy would have reacted.

In her book *Bird by Bird*, author Anne Lamott writes about her process of familiarizing herself with the characters in her novels. She uses an illustration borrowed from a friend of hers who presumably made their astute observations from watching people in real life.

According to Lamott, each of us has an acreage, or garden, that represents our personality. Within that space, we can choose to prune certain aspects while letting others go unrestricted. We can cultivate and grow one area while another remains undeveloped.[2]

---

2 Anne Lamott, *Bird by Bird* (New York, NY: Penguin Random House, 1994), 75–76.

This is a good description of personality which encompasses our reactions, sense of humour, preferences, and who we gel with and who we find tiresome. Our personalities are among the components that make us unique. Just as most backyards are different in size, shape, and layout, we are all profoundly different from one another.

When we think of the key characters of 1 Timothy, they seem to have very different acreages.

Paul is often portrayed as an abrasive, dogmatic individual who perhaps didn't prune enough of his Pharisee past when he adopted Christianity. This side of him was on display when the fundamentals of his Christian faith were undermined by false teaching. Here we see the uncompromising Paul who adopted firm stances against Jewish food restrictions, on equality for the Gentiles, and a refusal to allow works to be considered as additions to the perfect gift of the cross.

However, this was only one side of his acreage. He had a more gracious side, one which we saw in his letter to Philemon. We also see glimpses of it in his greetings to other Christians, in his praise of the Colossian church, and even here in his letters to Timothy.

Timothy was a dear friend to Paul and may have been his closest companion. They had met during Paul's second missionary journey as the apostle travelled through the interior of modern-day Turkey on his way to Troas and the Aegean Sea in the north of the Mediterranean.

It appears that Timothy's mother was keen that her son accompany the apostle and Silas on their mission. Timothy was probably in his late teens or early twenties by this time, ready to leave home and establish himself as a man.

Prior to leaving home, though, he underwent circumcision, presumably by Paul. No doubt the procedure affected their relationship. It was somewhat contentious given Paul's comments in Galatians 5:2.

Timothy's decision to undergo such a procedure displays his high level of commitment and willingness to trust his future mentor. It also shows significant faith on his part to believe that this most uncomfortable experience would be necessary for the good of the mission.

In these events, we see something of Timothy's character. We observe a brave young man who had been so convinced by the truth of the gospel that he was willing for Paul to operate on him. He was also willing to endure the subsequent pain as his wounds healed.

If the start to Timothy's mission was challenging, I expect his life on the road got no easier. He experienced many of the same troubles that beset Paul during those times.

Paul and Timothy travelled together on and off for almost twenty years (AD 49–68). At the time of Paul writing to him on this first occasion, Timothy was likely in his forties, in the midst of middle age. Thus for almost half his life Timothy had travelled or been on mission with Paul through Turkey, Macedonia, Greece, Italy, and Palestine.

It is likely they also worked in a trade together, for Paul was always encouraging Christians to have a means with which to pay their way. Whether Timothy was a fellow tentmaker, like Paul, we do not know. I would like to think of them working together, making plans for their next mission, and talking of their shared faith.

Initially we're presented with this steadfast side of Timothy's personality, loyal and courageous, brave and resolute. There is another side of him, though, one that Paul mentions when he encourages Timothy to take some wine to settle his stomach and prevent his frequent illnesses (1 Timothy 5:23). He also speaks in 2 Timothy to this quieter, timid side, encouraging Timothy to fan into flames the gift of God (2 Timothy 1:6). Paul tells him neither to be ashamed of the gospel nor to exhibit a spirit of timidity (2 Timothy 1:7).

Just like his mentor, Timothy had at least two sides to his acreage, two sides to his personality. A resolute, loyal side and a side that caused him to shy away from difficult tasks. Paul trusted Timothy, though, to cultivate the former and step away from the latter. Timothy evidently demonstrated that he was capable of doing so, giving Paul confidence that his disciple could work through some of the issues in Ephesus.

The church in Ephesus was the third character in the letters and apparently the acreage of the church needed some work. Metaphorically speaking some areas of the Ephesian church yard had become too wild. Paul was keen for Timothy to prune back some of the Ephesian excess that had developed.

Due to its position as a major port and a gateway to the East, Ephesus was multicultural and polytheistic. Such an environment predisposed to false teaching and a dilution of the purity of the gospel. One of the warning letters to the churches in Revelation was addressed to the church in Ephesus, and it regarded this very concern (Revelation 2:1–7). Timothy's role in the city was to tend to the church's acreage and bring it back into line with the gospel.

1 Timothy weaves between the controversial issues in the church and the continued mentoring of Timothy. It speaks to the commitment of Paul to the early Christians in Ephesus and the deep friendship between Paul and Timothy.

There are words here for us, too. Words, which if we can listen and apply to our own acreages might enable Christ-like fruits to flourish there.

Command

1 TIMOTHY 1:1-2

Paul, an apostle of Christ Jesus by the command of God our Savior and of Christ Jesus our hope,[2] To Timothy my true son in the faith: Grace, mercy and peace from God the Father and Christ Jesus our Lord.

We do not relish the prospect of being placed under the authority of others. We have an innate, hard to suppress drive to be independent.

Paul seemed to anticipate that there might be some reluctance among the rebellious factions of the Ephesian church, and maybe even from Timothy, to listen to his instructions. As such, he emphasized his own submission to God, highlighting in whose authority he wrote through the use of the word command in 1 Timothy 1:1.

In previous greetings Paul called himself an apostle by the will of God (1 and 2 Corinthians, Ephesians, and Colossians). Here, though, he stresses that he acted under the direct command of God. The Greek word *epitage* comes from the words *epi*, meaning "upon" or "over," and *tasso*, which is translated as "to order" or "arrange," the concept being that God has placed arrangements/ orders over or upon Paul.

Paul therefore felt that he had been authoritatively called by God.

On reflection, Paul's conversion was strikingly direct. Christ's voice and the blinding light arrested him on his journey to Damascus. And although Paul didn't shirk from his destination, his life was spiritually turned around and brought under Christ's authority.

Thirty years later, he still recalled the moment he had been seized by Christ's voice and allowed himself to come under Christ's command (Acts 9).

The direct command of God also conveyed to Paul the authority to act in God's name. Some may have questioned the credibility of Paul's apostleship, since he wasn't one of the original disciples and hadn't been present at the great commission. This might have undermined his claims to an apostle's authority, explaining why he emphasized his credentials, having received a command direct from the commanding officer, not through an intermediary or lesser official.

Not only was Paul an apostle, sent with the authority of another, he was also operating under a command given to him directly by that sending authority. His credentials therefore had a double certification.

I wonder whether Timothy's obedience and loyalty to Paul grew out of his respect for Paul's twofold credentials.

Timothy evidently respected his mentor and was adept at following his commands to travel to Ephesus and help remedy the growing pains of the church. Paul's greeting serves as a timely reminder to his disciple that, despite their clear earthly ties to one another, both of them had allegiances to a higher authority who commanded their respect and obedience.

At the beginning of this new study, we also have to be reminded that we are no longer the captain of our own hearts or souls. Our authority has been usurped by that of Christ and our will as Christians is to do His will.

APPLICATION: COMMAND

- When you are instructed by others or issued an instruction, consider that God too provides us with instruction. He expects our obedience, just as others will expect yours.
- We don't like coming under the authority of others. As you embark on this new study, pray that you would be willing to come under God's authority.
- Thank God for Timothy's willingness to accept leadership from Paul, and for Paul's willingness to come under the authority of Christ. Pray that you might accept the leadership of other Christians as well as Christ for guidance in your own life.

Pure Heart

1 TIMOTHY 1:3-7

As I urged you when I went into Macedonia, stay there in Ephesus so that you may command certain people not to teach false doctrines any longer [4] or to devote themselves to myths and endless genealogies. Such things promote controversial speculations rather than advancing God's work—which is by faith. [5] The goal of this command is love, which comes from a pure heart and a good conscience and a sincere faith. [6] Some have departed from these and have turned to meaningless talk. [7] They want to be teachers of the law, but they do not know what they are talking about or what they so confidently affirm.

According to Vine's Bible Dictionary, there are at least ten different Greek words for command.[3] We already encountered one of these in 1 Timothy 1:1, and we find another in today's reading. Why was so much commanding done in such a short passage?

---

3 "Command (Verbs)," *Studybible.info*. Date of access: October 21, 2023 (https://studybible.info/vines/Command%20(Verbs)).

Paul was perhaps responding to the urgency of the situation in Ephesus. Alternatively, it may have just been in his authoritarian nature to write in this manner. Or perhaps he needed to take a commanding tone to impress upon Timothy that a firm hand was called for.

It may be that all three were true. In fact, this seems most likely when reading the text.

Paul wrote firmly, and with urgency, instructing Timothy to quieten those who would spread false teaching. His tone reflects the depth of his feelings toward the purity of the gospel and the well-being of the Ephesian church.

The Ephesian church was dear to Paul, for it had been one of his early successes. He had mentored them through the Kindergarten stage of their faith and into early maturity, labouring amongst them for two to three years on an earlier missionary journey.

The time Paul personally invested in this church should have meant that they were well-equipped to detect heresy, due to the secure spiritual foundation built by Paul and his team. It seems, though, that although some respected Paul's teachings others had busied themselves chasing after mythologies and genealogies and following the Law for the Law's sake.

Paul directed Timothy to make advancing God's work the church's new or realigned priority (1 Timothy 1:4–5). They needed to take a new tack. This was important, since sailing off course by even a few degrees would distract them from pursuing God, preventing His work from being done.

Paul's goal of redirecting this body of believers is evidence of God's agape, or sacrificial, love at work. According to Paul, such love results from three components, all working toward the same end: a pure heart, a clear conscience, and a sincere faith (1 Timothy 1:5).

It's valuable to dwell on 1 Timothy 1:5, revisiting it whenever we face conflict or need to instruct one another. We can pay particular attention to the phrase "pure heart." It acts like a buffer to stop us in our tracks.

Paul accused those who pursued conflict of having impure hearts, their goals not being to pursue love from a pure heart, clear conscience, and sincere faith.

Like the Ephesians, we often pursue arguments or points of contention in order to convince others of our position. In doing so, we lose sight of one of the most important aspects of church life: we are God's stewards and we are to do His work with the goal of producing His love in others.

If we have a pure heart, *katharos kardia* in the Greek, our motive for instruction, discussion, and teaching the law is not to win, look good, or save face but rather to promote the genuine salvation of others.

When this is our sincere motive, our devotedness to our argument is less important than the individual or group we're in discussion with. Upholding them before God takes centre stage, knowing when to leave the discussion with Him, for His work is our goal.

Katharos kardia has an element of naivety, yet it also carries the granite-like certainty that we are doing God's work, and it will prevail. This confidence overcomes any perception of weakness from being naïve; rather, we rely on His strength out of a pure heart to accomplish His goals.

The word pure in Greek, *katharos,* references the unblemished high-karat metals that aren't tarnished or forged with other metals to form an alloy. The same word describes clothes that had been cleansed of any dirt or grime. Paul uses the word here to describe an unspoiled, uncorrupted heart. His writing has overtones of the beatitudes: *"Blessed are the pure in heart, for they will see God"* (Matthew 5:8).

At the outset of his letter to Timothy, Paul highlights the importance of a clean, unadulterated heart both in terms of a yardstick by which to measure the Ephesian teachers and as a standard for Timothy to aspire to.

Paul's words in 1 Timothy 1:5 aren't just timely for us to consider today. They're also worth reflecting on periodically throughout our lives. Let us endeavour not to be devoted to modern equivalents of genealogies and mythologies or be so stuck in the letter of the Law that we miss its purpose. Rather, we should pray that our hearts may be pure, secure in the knowledge that we are working as His stewards to do His will and engender His love in the lives of others.

APPLICATION: PURE HEART

- Consider your attitude about the word pure. Is it possible as adults to have hearts that aren't corrupted by our experiences? Pray that your motive for instructing others would be a sincere wish to see them blossom in God's love.

- When we dwell on an argument or contentious issue, part of our reluctance to "let go and let God" is due to impurities in our heart. Could this be true? Talk this over with God and ask Him to search your heart.
- In *katharos kardia*, a pure heart, we choose one of the components that Paul indicated would produce love. The other two, sincere faith and a clear conscience, are also important. So that all may function smoothly together, pray that God would refine all three of these components to enable you to be an effective teacher in whatever sphere God places you in.

Glorious Gospel

1 TIMOTHY 1:8–11

We know that the law is good if one uses it properly. [9] We also know that the law is made not for the righteous but for lawbreakers and rebels, the ungodly and sinful, the unholy and irreligious, for those who kill their fathers or mothers, for murderers, [10] for the sexually immoral, for those practicing homosexuality, for slave traders and liars and perjurers—and for whatever else is contrary to the sound doctrine [11] that conforms to the gospel concerning the glory of the blessed God, which he entrusted to me.

Shekinah is the Hebrew word used to describe the indescribable presence of God's glory on earth. Although not used in the Bible, it is thought to have been developed as a teaching aid during the intertestamental period. Shekinah emphasized the aura of the burning bush (Exodus 3), the awesome potency of God's passing presence as Moses hid behind a cleft in the rock (Exodus 33), and the reassuring pillar of cloud and fire that led the Israelites through the desert (Exodus 13).

This useful word speaks to God's magnificence, power, and lustrous brilliance. We encounter it as a blinding light when the

Ark of Covenant is depicted, or reflected on Moses's glowing face after he stood in the presence of God.

In modern times, this word has been adopted by the Christian church. It is accompanied by the word glory in the phrase "shekinah glory." The two words have the same meaning, but in repetition they create a stronger impression. The term has also been used to describe Jesus.

Shekinah glory presents an accurate word picture, rich in the potency of Christ's aura, healing power, perceptive teaching, and command over creation. It is Christ's life epitomized.

In today's passage, Paul reminded Timothy that some sins were obvious for Christians who had seen the light of Christ and the Law wasn't needed. However, the Law still has its use, just as spectacles have use for those whose vision remains impaired (1 Timothy 1:9–10).

False teaching, which is contrary to sound doctrine, emphasizes the importance of the Law and dulls the lustre of the glorious gospel. Dwelling on the glorious nature of Christ's life and that of His Father lifts these verses, reminding us to reflect upon the shekinah glory of Christ. As we pause on these images, we recall our prior life of stumbling along in our blindness. We remember anew our first glimpses of His glory. We experience afresh the beauty of seeing clearly under His dawning light and feel honoured to live in His presence.

APPLICATION: GLORIOUS GOSPEL

- Flat light occurs when the sun's light is blocked by clouds. This effect can make alpine skiing treacherous as the topography becomes ill-defined. Just as we need the sun's brightness to navigate a bumpy ski run, so too we need the glorious gospel to steer our paths through life.
- Pray for a fresh sunrise in your application of the gospel, so that the clouds will lift and your view of the brilliance of Christ will be restored.
- When you switch on a light today, take a moment to thank God for the gift of the glorious gospel.

Given Strength

1 TIMOTHY 1:12–17

I thank Christ Jesus our Lord, who has given me strength, that he considered me trustworthy, appointing me to his service. [13] Even though I was once a blasphemer and a persecutor and a violent man, I was shown mercy because I acted in ignorance and unbelief. [14] The grace of our Lord was poured out on me abundantly, along with the faith and love that are in Christ Jesus.

[15] Here is a trustworthy saying that deserves full acceptance: Christ Jesus came into the world to save sinners—of whom I am the worst. [16] But for that very reason I was shown mercy so that in me, the worst of sinners, Christ Jesus might display his immense patience as an example for those who would believe in him and receive eternal life. [17] Now to the King eternal, immortal, invisible, the only God, be honor and glory for ever and ever. Amen.

Paul usually gives his letters a purposeful structure. The introduction includes majestic theology to inspire the reader to dream. This is followed by instruction that brings his readers back down to earth.

Given Strength: 1 Timothy 1:12-17

In 1 Timothy, however, due to the personal nature of the correspondence, Paul employs less structure. It takes on a more patchwork quality, with bits of theology accompanied by both personal and corporate instruction for the Ephesian church. It's more typical of a letter a parent might write to a grown-up child to pass along advice and encouragement

Today's verses provide an example of Paul demonstrating his generous heart to his son in the faith. They highlight Paul's redeemed character, faithful commitment to Christ, and heartfelt desire to encourage similar characteristics in Timothy.

Consider for a moment Paul's goal in writing in such a personal fashion. Had he wanted to write directly to the church, we might instead have had a second letter to Ephesians. In such a letter, we might have broader correspondence with similar theological grounding and practical instruction as his other corporate letters.

Here, though, his intention is to be demonstrative to Timothy. Paul wanted to build into his dear colleague some of the life lessons he himself had experienced. Paul's goal was to nurture Timothy's character.

Paul didn't write with the expectation that his letter would be printed in the most published book of all time, nor did he write with the expectation that thousands or millions might read his words. The letter was a sincere gesture born from paternal love for his son in the faith. When we appreciate this, the verses are transformed into a personal message between individuals. Paul was giving Timothy another chance to hear his testimony.

There can be little doubt that Timothy had heard this before. My mischievous side imagines him smiling to himself as he read 1 Timothy 1:12, anticipating another rendition of a familiar story. Timothy might have had the same look in his eye that we have when we listen to yet another telling of an old anecdote.

In 1 Timothy 1:12, Paul writes that his own transformation was empowered by Christ. As Timothy wrestles with his character, as we all must, and faces off against some of the Ephesian believers, Paul reminds him that it is Christ who empowers our transformation, which of course has implications for both Timothy and the wayward Ephesians he must deal with.

The word given strength is taken from the Greek *endunamoo*, combining *en*, or "in," and *dunamoo*, meaning "strengthen" or "empower." We might picture Christ firing up a forge to transform a lump of metal into a useful tool, or perhaps providing the electrical current to enable the process of electrolysis, separating ore from its impurities.

What is the significance? The metal doesn't conjures the power to enable its own purification. The lump of steel doesn't manufacture the heat needed to enable its own forging into something useful.

So it is with Christian character; we are empowered to change by Him, not by our own manufactured enthusiasm.

Today's verses mark Paul's transition from a self-deprecating monologue into a genuine attempt to express wonderment at the majesty of God, who personally stooped down to gather Paul up and change his character from a lump of useless material and turning him into a fine instrument.

Paul's purpose was to inspire Timothy into reflecting on the amazing character of God, who had demonstrated His love not just in giving his Son but in the continuous provision of power needed to transform our self-centredness into Christ-centred nobility. Once we grasp this, we too can readily adopt Paul's words of praise that so eloquently reflect his gratitude.

Jesus words from Luke 7:47 resonant loudly with Paul's purpose: *"Therefore, I tell you, her many sins have been forgiven—as her great love has shown. But whoever has been forgiven little loves little."*

In order to grow into the character Christ would have us adopt, we need to better understand who saved us. We must grasp the magnitude of Christ's grace to draw us away from the being the worst of sinners. Through this process, we will become more grateful and empowered to mirror His grace in our lives.

We often don't have Paul's perspective on this—or, for that matter, the perspective of Christ and His Father. A touch more humility is required if we are to achieve the transformation we confess to desire.

APPLICATION: GIVEN STRENGTH

- It is illogical to demonstrate weakness in order to grow in strength of character. Humbly come before God to acknowledge your weaknesses and need for His strength.
- Reflect on your own attempts to be self-disciplined, then reflect on the majesty of the immortal, invisible

King and recommit to being His follower instead of your own life coach.

• Thank God for His grace by reflecting on Luke 7 and the woman from Simon's house. What can we learn from her example?

You are going to have to give and give and give, or there's no reason for you to be writing. You have to give from the deepest part of yourself, and you are going to have to go on giving, and the giving is going to have to be its own reward. There is no cosmic importance to your getting something published, but there is in learning to be a giver.[4]

—Anne Lamott

---

4 Lamott, *Bird by Bird*, 252.

Holding On to Faith

1 TIMOTHY 1:18-20

Timothy, my son, I am giving you this command in keeping with the prophecies once made about you, so that by recalling them you may fight the battle well, [19] holding on to faith and a good conscience, which some have rejected and so have suffered shipwreck with regard to the faith. [20] Among them are Hymenaeus and Alexander, whom I have handed over to Satan to be taught not to blaspheme.

Paul wraps up 1 Timothy 1 by referring back to his opening instructions. He emphasizes the imagery he is trying to portray by writing on the theme of fighting the battle of faith.

He refers to the commandment he instructed Timothy to undertake in 1 Timothy 1:3: *"command certain people not to teach false doctrines any longer or to devote themselves to myths and endless genealogies."*

According 1 Timothy 1:18, Timothy should feel capable and competent in the task. To aid him in his role, Timothy received gifts that were revealed in prophecies about him. He was also encouraged to hold on to the faith and keep a good conscience (1 Timothy 1:19).

Whether or not we possess similar gifts, we will need to hold on to the faith and maintain a good conscience if we are to keep ourselves on track with Him in our secular world.

Holding on to the faith is a familiar term, although it's likely overlooked or dismissed as an important strategy against false teaching.

Paul used the word *echon*, which means "holding," although it can also refer to "having" or "possessing." In 1 Timothy 1:19, the word faith is not accompanied by an article in its first use, but it is in the second. As such, "the faith" has been understood to refer to one's confidence and assurance in Jesus, since He is the author and perfecter of our faith (Hebrews 12:2).

Holding on to Jesus for reassurance would have been important to Timothy. He didn't have the advantage of having some of the same resources we have today in the fight against false teachers. For example, he wouldn't have had the benefit of the gospels.

Instead his image of Christ would have been brought to life through the time he spent with Paul, Silas, and others. These experiences and ongoing instruction from the Holy Spirit would have been immensely important in building his faith, a faith he would need to draw upon in his day-to-day challenge of pitting secular values versus Christian ones and confronting the misdirection of the false teachers.

Time and again in his letters, Paul encouraged his readers to return, renew, and revisit their assurance in Jesus. He employed this approach in so many different situations: to heighten our worship, bring us to prayer, maintain our purity in conflict, and strengthen our resolve.

Paul repeatedly draws on the miracle of Christian conversion to remind us of who we serve, what resources are available to us, and to what we are being called. By holding on to the faith, by returning to Christ, our consciences are cleared, and remain clear, as we operate in the world.

False teaching probably looks different today than it did in the first century, yet the potential for us to drift from our anchor of true faith persists. Timothy had a solid understanding of what it looked like to remain moored; he had observed Paul for more than twenty years. Paul had ridden out many storms in his ministry yet hadn't left the harbour of the faith.

Paul reminded Timothy to hold on to Christ so the campaign to which he had been called in Ephesus could be fought and not shipwrecked.

As we consider what it looks like for us to hold onto the faith, what comes to mind? Hopefully spending time in His word is part of this picture, as would being involved with a church that's in tune with the gospel. We should probably also seek like-minded partners in our ministries, just like Paul and Timothy did.

There are other components to a person's faithful walk. However, at a core level, we need to be tethered tightly to an accurate image of Christ. This can only be achieved through personal relationship, brokered at conversion, maintained through prayer, and sustained through a clear conscience. Paul would urge us to hold to this image daily so we can fight the good fight.

APPLICATION: HOLDING ON TO FAITH

- Picture a boat bobbing in the harbour tied to a mooring. We are tied to Christ, our anchor. Refresh your ties with Him and secure your anchorage by thanking Him for His grace to save you.
- Having faith means being confident in what we hope for and assured about what we do not see (Hebrews 11:1). Pray for confidence in knowing Christ so you may be able to declare, like Paul, *"I know whom I have believed"* (2 Timothy 1:12).
- It's possible to be deceived and hold on to the wrong image of the faith. Pray that you, and the global Christian community, would remain true to the faith.

Intercession

I urge, then, first of all, that petitions, prayers, intercession and thanksgiving be made for all people—² for kings and all those in authority, that we may live peaceful and quiet lives in all godliness and holiness. ³ This is good, and pleases God our Savior, ⁴ who wants all people to be saved and to come to a knowledge of the truth. ⁵ For there is one God and one mediator between God and mankind, the man Christ Jesus, ⁶ who gave himself as a ransom for all people. This has now been witnessed to at the proper time. ⁷ And for this purpose I was appointed a herald and an apostle—I am telling the truth, I am not lying—and a true and faithful teacher of the Gentiles.

In these opening lines of 1 Timothy 2, I wonder whether Paul, having growled out strong statements regarding Hymenaeus and Alexander and false teachers, doesn't self-consciously catch himself and turn to prayer as a remedy.

Instead of continuing on a tirade, he reminds himself and Timothy of the importance of praying for rulers and authority figures, whether they are false teachers or not. He mentions many types of supplication we should make: petitions, petitions, prayers, intercessions, and thanksgivings. This explains how broad our ministrations can be as we hold others in our thoughts before God.

The breadth of such prayer is important. In asking, hoping, advocating, and being grateful, we cover tremendous ground in terms of our emotional involvement in tense issues.

For example, we might petition God for a new perspective on an individual. Our prayer for that person could progress as we hope for a resolution to their crisis though a God-given intervention. We might also advocate or intercede for another before God in order to bring about reconciliation. Finally, following Paul's pattern, we could give thanks for the individuals in authority who challenge us.

Paul didn't just provide a clever string of synonyms for prayer. We can use this list as a formula to lift us from potentially dark thoughts—such as Paul's toward Hymenaeus and Alexander—to the more peaceful outlook he arrives at by the end of 1 Timothy 2:2.

In that state of mind, like Paul, we might remember that it is God's desire that all should be saved and come to a knowledge of the truth.

In the original Greek, *enteuxeis* is the word that's translated here as "intercession." It has been translated as petition in some versions. Either way, it communicates a definite sense of one person making a request on behalf of another. When we intercede, we advocate on behalf of someone else.

The concept of interceding for others calls to mind the second greatest commandment:

"Teacher, which is the greatest commandment in the Law?"

Jesus replied: "'Love the Lord your God with all your heart and with all your soul and with all your mind.' This is the first and greatest commandment. And the second is like it: 'Love your neighbor as yourself.' All the Law and the Prophets hang on these two commandments." (Matthew 22:36–40)

If the golden commandment is to love God, the silver one is for us to love our neighbours. Paul reminded Timothy, and us, to be conscious of this in our prayers, that we might intercede on behalf of neighbours to our heavenly Father. Praying for the needs of others, whether we're at peace or in conflict with them, is a sobering way to lift ourselves from anger or redirect our thoughts from our own private interests.

When we intercede for others in prayer, as Paul suggests in 1 Timothy 2:1, we obey the silver commandment. We also demonstrate Christ-like behaviour and mirror in a small way His intercession for us before His Father.

In our daily prayers, we should remember to intercede for others more often, so we may be lifted from our own pools of self-reflection to see things from His perspective.

APPLICATION: INTERCESSION

- Who do you pray for regularly? What do you intercede for on their behalf? How can you more effectively intercede for them?
- Intercession was part of a four-pronged prayer strategy; petition, prayer (godly wishes), and thanksgiving were the other parts. Consider the structure of your own prayers and whether you could adopt this pattern.
- The Bible was written by godly people interceding on our behalf to enable us to receive God-inspired wisdom. As you open your Bible, use the opportunity as a prompt to intercede for others.

So once a year, when we went to the beach for our family vacation, I used those cherished early morning hours before anyone else was up to spend time with God making a master prayer list. I would sit and gaze out over the ocean, pencil and paper in hand, and ask God to show me how to pray for each child over the next twelve months… God always met me there with good instructions, and I came home with prayer lists for each of my children. Then throughout the year, I added to them whenever I needed to do so.[5]

—Stormie Omartian

5 Stormie Omartian, *The Power of a Praying Parent* (Eastbourne, UK: Kingsway Publications, 2000), 20.

Modestly

1 TIMOTHY 2:8–15

Therefore I want the men everywhere to pray, lifting up holy hands without anger or disputing. ⁹ I also want the women to dress modestly, with decency and propriety, adorning themselves, not with elaborate hairstyles or gold or pearls or expensive clothes, ¹⁰ but with good deeds, appropriate for women who profess to worship God.

¹¹ A woman should learn in quietness and full submission. ¹² I do not permit a woman to teach or to assume authority over a man; she must be quiet. ¹³ For Adam was formed first, then Eve. ¹⁴ And Adam was not the one deceived; it was the woman who was deceived and became a sinner. ¹⁵ But women will be saved through childbearing—if they continue in faith, love and holiness with propriety.

One night, Anne Lamott and her young son, Sam, walked up their driveway with a group of dinner guests to find someone's car. It was one of those crisp, clear nights that come in spring and fall when the stars seem to be in reach and the pines have their own kind of new cologne to share with the world. Didn't it smell wonderful?

"It smells like moon," Sam declared.

Perhaps he was making an association with a childhood memory of this smell of pines combined with a big, bright moon.[6]

I share this anecdote to provide some perspective on today's verses, which may at first provoke negative emotions. If we are to find peace for our consciences, we will need to take in some of the spring pine fragrance of the moon to settle any negativity that may have arisen.

These verses are inflammatory to our gender-sensitive ears. We have grown up in a culture where such a blatant demarcation of roles for men and women is frowned upon and dismissed as discrimination.

Much has been written about 1 Timothy 2:8–15. There are essentially two camps: those who emphasize the exegesis of the passage and rely on the patriarchy of Scripture, and those who emphasize the context into which Paul was writing. This context included goddess worship and a population of women who were discouraged from learning.

Before we look carefully at 1 Timothy 2:11–15, we will consider 1 Timothy 2:8–10.

Paul wrote about some of his personal preferences in church etiquette. The passage begins with the verb "want," in the New International Version, but in the original the word's meaning hews closer to "desire." Paul wasn't issuing a command. He was only

---

6 Lamott, *Bird by Bird*, 184.

expressing that certain behaviours in church sat better with his conscience.

Remember how important it is for teachers to hold to the faith and a good conscience (1 Timothy 1:5, 19). One's conscience is a combination of their cultural background, social experiences, and the guidance of the Holy Spirit.

When Paul was growing up, he would have witnessed men holding their empty hands up to God as sign of humble obedience and openness in the Jewish synagogue. As a result of this cultural upbringing, his conscience enjoys seeing the same behaviour in the Christian church. It resonated with his cultural and social experiences, all the while seeming to be in keeping with what the Holy Spirit desired.

1 Timothy 2:9 addresses the attitude of women when they pray. Paul's preference was for women to dress modestly and discretely, highlighting their inclusion in the service and prayer. We should not imagine that a dress code was intended to subjugate or demean the female sex. Men too were expected to dress modestly and discretely.

From these verses, we could dwell on the word modestly. And if we approach 1 Timothy 2:11–15 with modest hearts, I suspect some of the heat can be taken out of these statements. The original Greek word here is *aidous*, which has been translated as "unpretentiousness" or "reverence." The preferred attire for women (and men) would demonstrate respect for God. In Paul's eyes, the way one dressed in church was not meant to be a fashion statement.

If we approach 1 Timothy 2:11–12 modestly, with careful reflectiveness, we can note that the original refers not to "quietness" but "calmness," and not "full submission" but "under obedience." Both calmness and obedience are required if we are to learn from God's word. They would also be required by any honest male learner, who could no sooner learn with a jittery mind or rebellious heart than a woman could.

Although 1 Timothy 2:12 is problematic, it might reflect Paul's concern for husbands with domineering wives, since the terms man and woman could also be translated as husband and wife.

The type of authority Paul wrote about here is not the kind of authority a Christian woman would want to yield. The word used by Paul is *authentein*, and it's unusual. It was used to describe mastery of another for personal gain, as though sucking the life out of someone. It might be suggested that this isn't a quality any teacher, male or female, should aspire to.

The word quiet in 1 Timothy 2:12 is the same word used for quietness in the previous verse. Again, it emphasizes the importance of a calmness, or stillness, in church.

We can therefore conclude that 1 Timothy 2:12 does not prevent women from teaching in church.

Importantly, we must remember that 1 Timothy 2:11–12 are not the eleventh and twelfth commandments. They are Paul's preferences, reflecting his conscience, which in turn reflected both his Jewish heritage and the teaching of the Holy Spirit. Since they are not commandments, we should not allow them to become divisive issues. We must not lose sight of the fact that it is neither praying nor teaching that saves us; rather, it is Jesus.

Perhaps this is why Paul emphasized sanctification in the last few verses of the chapter.

We are not to infer from 1 Timothy 2:15 that women are saved through childbirth. This would be a falsehood, just as it's false to conclude that circumcision is a prerequisite for salvation. Christ alone is sufficient; His sacrifice does not require any additions. His life was payment enough. Our salvation, of men and women, was secured on the cross and not by our deeds.

The text of 1 Timothy 2:15 either refers to *the* childbirth, or the birth of Christ, as the original Greek used the definitive article. This may be interpreted to refer to Mary as a second Eve, bearing a blessing for women and all mankind by bearing and mothering Christ.

Alternatively, it may reflect the sanctification of parenthood.

Modestly, I would suggest the latter is true for men and women, mothers and fathers. Both parents need to work together if they are to raise children in a godly manner. In this, there are clear parallels to the selflessness required to raise children and the selflessness Christians grow into through sanctification.

By applying this verse generally to parenting, it can be read as an encouragement for parents who aren't able to have their own children. In such challenging circumstances, one's willingness to trust God and walk with Him through fostering or adoption can be even more demanding than having one's own children.

Rather than taking these verses at face value, with their heat and intensity, I would encourage the reader to look at what is behind the verses.

Paul wanted Timothy to see Jesus in the behaviour of the Christians in Ephesus. He hoped that Christ would be seen in their reverent prayer, respectful attire, and godly behaviour. The church should reflect Christ's glory, just as the moon is a reflection of the sun, and just as Paul himself tried to be a reflection of Christ.

These verses were written to encourage modesty, discretion, and orderliness in worship. The aim of the passage was not to divide but to unite worshippers, male and female alike.

Although we might miss it, there is diplomacy here. The language might obscure Paul's intention to reflect Christ, but Christ's reflection is there. Paul's awkward words are like clouds obscuring the moon and masking some of its shine. We can be sure of this, for Paul would not write for any other purpose.

Read this passage again in light of our meditations and see whether in hindsight you cannot "smell the moon." Christ's essence is there, present in the calls for open, empty hands, modesty, calmness, stillness, and non-manipulative teaching. It is there in the call for other-centredness as we mirror selflessness to our children.

Paul had high hopes for the Ephesians. He hoped they wouldn't just be shallow reflections of Christ or even a crescent-shaped moon; he hoped they would be a huge, bright, new moon that shone by example in everything they did.

APPLICATION: MODESTLY

• These verses serve as a reminder that we may not fully know God's ways until we are with Him in heaven.

Ask Him to renew a modest heart within you so you might earnestly follow Him.

• How do you pray? Take a look at your palms and open them wide. See that they are empty. When we come before God in prayer, He does not ask for a sacrifice or a gift; He asks only for willing, modest hands offered with a clear, clean conscience. Let this thought lead you to pray.

• God did design men and women to be different, to have different roles and fulfill different purposes. Society struggles with this, as does the church. Today's verses require reflection. When faced with strong opinions on passages like today's, remember to be modest. Take a deep breath to inhale the pine fragrance and smell the moon.

Let the morning bring me word of your unfailing love, for I have put my trust in you. Show me the way I should go, for to you I entrust my life. (Psalm 143:8)

Aspire

1 TIMOTHY 3:1-7

Here is a trustworthy saying: Whoever aspires to be an overseer desires a noble task. [2] Now the overseer is to be above reproach, faithful to his wife, temperate, self-controlled, respectable, hospitable, able to teach, [3] not given to drunkenness, not violent but gentle, not quarrelsome, not a lover of money. [4] He must manage his own family well and see that his children obey him, and he must do so in a manner worthy of full respect. [5] (If anyone does not know how to manage his own family, how can he take care of God's church?) [6] He must not be a recent convert, or he may become conceited and fall under the same judgment as the devil. [7] He must also have a good reputation with outsiders, so that he will not fall into disgrace and into the devil's trap.

The word aspire comes from the Greek, *oregetai*, meaning "to reach after" or "to yearn for." It speaks to the attitude of eagerness expected of a church overseer.

An overseer was to watch over the church. As such, their authority was in lieu of the higher authority of an apostle. If we look further up the chain of command, their role was as watchmen for Christ. In the New Testament, the term overseer is used interchangeably with elder. This evokes the image of a wise, older individual who brings sobriety and sound judgment to the task of fostering community.

To visualize an overseer, you could call to mind the image of a shepherd watching over his flock. This same image has subsequently given rise to the use of word "pastors" to describe overseers.

In ancient times, secular overseers were employed on building projects to watch over the progress of the work and bring it to completion, answerable to the project's benefactor.

When we understand what's involved in overseeing a church, taking responsibility for God's work and being held responsible to Him, we grasp something of the lofty aspiration required to undertake this role. It can be a disheartening quest, for only few can satisfy these formidable demands. Here we begin to feel something of the aspiration paradox that is the Christian's lot.

We aspire to hold to these qualities, knowing they will please our heavenly Father and give evidence of our love for Christ (John 14:21). We also know that we will fail (Romans 7:15). Further, we know that we will never achieve righteousness through our own works.

So why do we aspire to these tasks?

We aspire for in our aspiration we express our acknowledgement of the precious nature of God's grace. We aspire to the life

Paul describes, because we recognize how blessed we are. Our aspiration embodies our appreciation.

Those who stop aspiring treat grace with cheapness. The person who acknowledges sin but makes no attempt to change holds grace with contempt. They hold to a philosophy that grace will always be present to the confessing Christian, so why not use it often and without an afterthought?

Dietrich Bonhoeffer, in his book *The Cost of Discipleship*, begins by distinguishing costly grace from cheap grace. His assertion is simple: in making discipleship easy, or worldly, we devalue grace.[7]

When I read the list of qualities to be found in a person chosen to undertake church responsibilities, I feel deflated. I know how few will qualify. Paul knew this too.

More important than these qualities, though, is the attitude that fires a person's aspiration to exemplify them.

The aspiration paradox is that we might not achieve these qualities, but striving for them with honest and repentant hearts speaks to our understanding of the value of pure grace. In aspiring for discipleship, we acknowledge the magnitude of the gift that was bestowed upon us. With His gift, and our aspiring hearts, responsibilities in church, whether as an overseer or dishwasher, become natural extensions of our appreciative lives.

---

7 Dietrich Bonhoeffer, *The Cost of Discipleship* (New York, NY: Touchstone, 1995), 43–56.

APPLICATION: ASPIRE

- We read the Bible to be inspired by God, lifted from the world's ways to see a different way we can aspire to. Thank Him today for His word and for the inspiration it brings.
- We aspire to become more sanctified in our lives due to our growing appreciation of the depth of His grace. Take a moment to thank God for His Son, who enabled us to be redeemed.
- Consider a pillar. Acknowledge your lowly position by any standard of holiness based on our own works. Then look toward the high ceilings we can reach only through Christ. Renew your aspiration to lead a life that reflects your calling and understanding of the cost of grace.

Perhaps we had once heard the gracious call to follow him and had at this command even taken the first few streps along the path of discipleship in the discipline of obedience, only to find ourselves confronted by the word of cheap grace. Was that not merciless and hard? The only effect that such a word could have on us was to bar our way to progress, and seduce us to the mediocre level of the world, quenching the joy of discipleship by telling us that we were following a way of our own choosing, that were spending our strength and discipling ourselves in vain—all if which was not merely useless, but extremely dangerous. Afterall, we were told, our salvation had already been accomplished by the grace of God … The word of cheap grace has been the ruin of more Christians than any commandment of works.[8]

—Dietrich Bonhoeffer

8 Ibid., 54–55.

Service

In the same way, deacons are to be worthy of respect, sincere, not indulging in much wine, and not pursuing dishonest gain. ⁹ They must keep hold of the deep truths of the faith with a clear conscience. ¹⁰ They must first be tested; and then if there is nothing against them, let them serve as deacons.

¹¹ In the same way, the women are to be worthy of respect, not malicious talkers but temperate and trustworthy in everything.

¹² A deacon must be faithful to his wife and must manage his children and his household well. ¹³ Those who have served well gain an excellent standing and great assurance in their faith in Christ Jesus.

We don't associate service as a gift from our heavenly Father, but 1 Timothy 3:13 implants the idea that service could be a treasure that's rich in blessing and favour.

We would probably rank other blessings from discipleship much higher. Up near the top of the list would be being loved by God (John 3:16), being highly valued (Matthew 10:31), or being adopted into His God's family (Ephesians 1:5). Other highly appreciated treasures would be receiving the Holy Spirit (Ephesians 1:13) and being given purpose (Ephesians 2:10).

We perceive service as being menial, a necessary discipline, a required chore… something we know we must do but not something we relish.

The word deacon in the above verses is derived from the Greek word *diakoneo*, meaning "to wait" or "to serve." A deacon was someone who served under the authority of another. The deacon could be a waiter acting on the authority of their host, or an attendant carrying out the orders of their manager.

If we focus on the list of character attributes recommended for deacons, we may find that we don't measure up to Paul's standards. This would be disappointing, since our human nature never wants us to feel left out. We don't like to feel rejected or unworthy. This fear of missing out makes us anxious. We can even get judgmental towards those who've been chosen ahead of us.

Of course, this isn't the point of Paul's list, nor is it the point of the position of deacon. We should no sooner strive for either to embody these character traits without the accompanying character or to perform service without the appropriate serving heart.

To participate in church service, the first step is to pray that our hearts might be changed so service becomes a natural extension of our new nature, our rebirth in Christ. We acknowledge that we might not always feel like serving, even with new hearts, but we serve because we know it will bring joy to our hearts and others.

Paul and Timothy chose deacons for the church in Ephesus, but they would have hoped that such individuals almost chose themselves. They would have looked for individuals who were already acting in deacon-like ways to enable the church to reach its community. These would have been individuals who had already begun to demonstrate outward signs of their new Christian nature, those who had learnt from experience that good service brings its own reward (1 Timothy 3:13).

We've already discussed discipleship, a theme central in Paul's pastoral letters written to Timothy and Titus. Like them, we too follow in Christ's footsteps. So when we encounter a list of attributes such as in today's passage, whether we harbour designs on being a church deacon or not, we would do well to reflect on them in the manner of Psalm 139:23–24. I'm sure Timothy did.

As disciples of Christ, we are called to serve. But we are also called to straighten out any of our behaviours that wouldn't be becoming of an ambassador for Christ or deacon of the church.

APPLICATION: SERVICE

- Pray that through these verses, your understanding of church duties would be clarified so you can approach service as Christ did.
- Before our hearts change to see service differently, we may need to sow a habit to pray weekly, or daily, for Christ's servant heart.
- You may already be devotedly serving in your church. May God bless you for this. May He also enable you to share your service with others. Pray for service partners who will readily and in a godly manner support you in your works.

Sing

1 TIMOTHY 3:14–16

Although I hope to come to you soon, I am writing you these instructions so that, [15] if I am delayed, you will know how people ought to conduct themselves in God's household, which is the church of the living God, the pillar and foundation of the truth. [16] Beyond all question, the mystery from which true godliness springs is great: He appeared in the flesh, was vindicated by the Spirit, was seen by angels, was preached among the nations, was believed on in the world, was taken up in glory.

Rather than just expressing himself in words, Paul writes in a way that not only expresses his praise and thanks but also contains a poetic style. These words almost seem to form a hymn.

Something happens emotionally when we sing. Words become more meaningful, and our thoughts are cleared of distractions. We focus on the moment, whatever that moment might be, whether we're in the shower, driving the car, or sitting in church. Other distractions dissolve as we subconsciously follow the tune and sing the lyrics.

We sing out in response to our emotions, hopefully joyous ones, in a desire to express our ourselves. There is an emotional release. And in these verses, Paul lyrically expresses his joy. We can experience the emotion with him in song.

Having identified the key characteristics needed for someone to serve in church, Paul now takes a moment to sit back and remembers what an amazing blessing it is to be writing to a new Christian church. He considers how far the gospel has spread, the lives it has touched and changed. In this moment, his heart is moved. The emotions stir and he needs to give thanks and acknowledge Christ—Christ the mystery, Christ the man, Christ the Son of God, He who was rejected but is now seated with God. In this enigma, Paul has no answer but to sing in response to the awe and wonder of his heart.

Paul's song expresses something of his change of perspective as he considers the church in Ephesus. He transitions from acknowledging his concerns that he might be delayed to appreciating that God has these concerns in hand. He realizes in the marrow of his being, in the fibre of his bone and steel of his spirit, that God will help secure the personnel Timothy needs for his elders and deacons. God will supply the workers for His household and provide the strength Timothy needs to complete his tasks. This appreciation leads him to express his joy in the mystery that is God and the revelation that is Christ.

What makes you sing? Physiologically, you breathe out against your vocal cords, causing them to vibrate. But this doesn't explain what motivates you. Perhaps it's more specific to ask, what *moves* you to sing? From where do you find the drive? What emotions lead you to smile with your voice?

Like Paul, we find joy from remembering all that Christ was and is. We may also find joy in creation or in seeing Christ come to life in others.

Read Paul's lyrics again in 1 Timothy 3:16 and see whether they make you smile. This emotion, appreciating the joy of Christ anew, doesn't need to be reserved for Christmas mornings.

APPLICATION: SING

- When you find yourself smiling this week, consider that it's your soul singing and giving thanks to God for the joy He brings.
- At church, take a moment during praise to breathe in the occasion. Thank God for the voices, the music, the musicians, and the hearts that are expressing their appreciation of His mystery.
- Paul went from expressing an anxiety to singing an anthem. Singing has a way of calming hearts. David and the psalmist do it regularly in the Psalms. Try it this week with the accompaniment of your favourite praise artist—or if you're feeling brave, in a solo.

Extraordinary Godliness

1 TIMOTHY 4:1-10

The Spirit clearly says that in later times some will abandon the faith and follow deceiving spirits and things taught by demons. [2] Such teachings come through hypocritical liars, whose consciences have been seared as with a hot iron. [3] They forbid people to marry and order them to abstain from certain foods, which God created to be received with thanksgiving by those who believe and who know the truth. [4] For everything God created is good, and nothing is to be rejected if it is received with thanksgiving, [5] because it is consecrated by the word of God and prayer.

[6] If you point these things out to the brothers and sisters, you will be a good minister of Christ Jesus, nourished on the truths of the faith and of the good teaching that you have followed. [7] Have nothing to do with godless myths and old wives' tales; rather, train yourself to be godly. [8] For physical training is of some value, but godliness has value for all things, holding promise for both the present life and the life to come. [9] This is a trustworthy saying that deserves full

acceptance. [10] That is why we labor and strive, because we have put our hope in the living God, who is the Savior of all people, and especially of those who believe.

Whenwaves reach the shore, we watch them roll up the beach. We note their approach like marching troops, arriving in line after line.

If we look more closely, though, we will be able to glimpse occasional waves that move in a different direction from the others, perpendicular to the proverbial marching troops. These hidden waves run at ninety degrees to the tide and are caused by the collision of two of the marching waves. Their movement can be hidden from the casual observer, so you might be deceived into believing they don't exist.

Deception is often like this. Without being circumspect, a lie can be readily overlooked and hidden from plain sight.

In these verses, Paul alerts Timothy to the dangers of deception. Deception in the church, like an unseen wave, is often the result of an energetic new teaching or perspective. How can we determine when inspirational leadership is God inspired and not misguided?

Paul suggested to Timothy that training in godliness is a good antidote against being misled by godless myths and traditional stories (1 Timothy 4:7). He spoke from personal experience, having previously been deceived by the false energies of the Pharisees and carried away in a direction that led away from the kingdom of God.

Paul missed who Christ was and failed to understand the march of the biblical teachings all indicating that Christ was the

Messiah. His deception should be a warning to all Christians to be wary of the direction of their faith.

However, training in Christian godliness must have come to mean something different to Paul, since ostensibly he had been trained in godliness his whole life.

Godliness as a word has lost some of its saltiness and emphasis. If you have a church background, the word is overfamiliar. To train in godliness does not sound aspirational.

In the second part of *The Cost of Discipleship*, Bonhoeffer leads the reader through the Sermon on the Mount in Matthew 5–7. He specifically discusses Matthew 5:48, which says, *"Be perfect, therefore, as your heavenly Father is perfect."*

If we summarize Bonhoeffer's thoughts, it becomes clear that the word "perfect" means extraordinary in this beatitude and is an allusion to an ideal of Christian maturity.[9]

Christian maturity is the fruit of our training in godliness and it is how we become extra-ordinary. Being extra-ordinary sounds more aspirational as a defence against deception. Although becoming extra-ordinary sounds exciting, the humbling truth of 1 Timothy 4:7–10 is that training in godliness requires us to put our hope in God, for He is our Saviour.

When we perceive that we don't need Him, as with the Pharisees, we trust our own devices and become deceived. Thus, in order to train in godliness and rise above the bland to become extraordinary (Matthew 5:47–48), the first and main step in our journey is to acknowledge His lordship (1 Timothy 4:10).

---

9 Ibid., 154.

APPLICATION: EXTRAORDINARY GODLINESS

- Like the unseen sideways waves on the beach that cut across the tide, we can easily miss deception due to its hidden nature. Prayerfully ask God to bring to your attention areas of deception in your life.
- Is there more room in your life for the extraordinary? There always is. Rather than wallowing in personal failures, let's be buoyed by His grace and not be sidelined by deceptive thoughts.
- If godliness is about being extraordinary, it becomes a character trait of interest. Use that as a prod to motivative you to revisit the Sermon on the Mount (Matthew 5–6). It's a challenging message, but these words of Christ are wise. They remain an excellent syllabus for our training in Christian godliness.

Persevere

Command and teach these things. [12] Don't let anyone look down on you because you are young, but set an example for the believers in speech, in conduct, in love, in faith and in purity. [13] Until I come, devote yourself to the public reading of Scripture, to preaching and to teaching. [14] Do not neglect your gift, which was given you through prophecy when the body of elders laid their hands on you.

[15] Be diligent in these matters; give yourself wholly to them, so that everyone may see your progress. [16] Watch your life and doctrine closely. Persevere in them, because if you do, you will save both yourself and your hearers.

Renowned author Malcolm Gladwell wrote a book, *David and Goliath*, that discusses instances when short defeats tall, small overcomes great, and minor overwhelms major. In its third chapter, Gladwell writes about instances when size influences perseverance. His observations are thought-provoking and relevant to the verses above as Paul addresses Timothy's staying power (1 Timothy 4:16).

Gladwell takes note of the difference in perseverance between undergraduates of similar capabilities, depending on whether they attend an academically weak university versus a higher-achieving school. Those at weaker universities persevere to the end of their degree in greater numbers than those at Ivy league institutions.

He proposes that this stems from an undergraduate's perceived success. The encouragement they receive from their performance in projects, grades, exams, and classwork motivates them to keep trying.

Modest students at elite schools perceive that they are underachieving, then become discouraged and give up. In contrast, modest students in lower academic centres persevere through encouragement and a personal sense of achievement to complete their goals.[10]

In 1 Timothy 4:16, Paul causes Timothy, and us, to reflect on the components of perseverance. If we think about what prompts us not to give up, I suspect that we will find truth in Gladwell's observations. Perception of success is strong component in one's willingness to persevere. Perception of success is an encourager.

If we consider today's passage from 1 Timothy, Paul implores Timothy to persevere by reminding him of his calling into Christian ministry (1 Timothy 4:14). He acknowledges Timothy's gifting to slay metaphorical bears and lions. Timothy's calling had a holy ordinance, a spiritual blessing.

10 Malcolm Gladwell, *David and Goliath* (New York, NY: Back Bay Books, 2013), 63–96.

Paul also added a word of personal encouragement to strengthen Timothy's resolve. Encouragement is therefore not only significant in the secular environment. Christians also benefit from having cheerleaders.

Timothy would have struggled to persevere in the environment he was working in. The Christian church was the David of religious organizations at that time, like the small shepherd boy confronting the Goliath of the Jewish religion. Timothy needed strength in his spirit, body, and arm if he was to persevere in the work before him.

In *The Pilgrim's Progress*, Christian gets mired in the Slough of Despond. His travelling companion, Pliable, becomes discouraged and turns back towards Destruction. Christian, though, continues on, struggling in the boggy ground.

How did he persevere through despondency? He persevered due to his belief in his pilgrimage and the appearance of another character who arrived on the scene, named Help. Help brought words of encouragement and pulled Christian out of the mire by hand.[11]

The character of Christian persevered by having faith in his mission, but he was certainly grateful for that encouraging hand from Help.

---

11 John Bunyan, *The Pilgrim's Progress* (Minneapolis, MN: Desiring God, 2014), 9–12.

APPLICATION: PERSEVERE

- The word persevere is translated from *epimene* in Greek. It can be broken down into *epi*, meaning "on, at, or in," and *meo*, meaning "to stay, remain, or endure." When we persevere, we actively choose to remain. This implies sustained effort. Pray God that would remind you of your calling and gifts to encourage you in those tasks that need perseverance.
- Think of someone who might need your encouragement today. Consider Help, pulling Christian from the mire of despondency. Is there an opportunity for you to bring some sunshine to someone you know?
- Gladwell's observations are insightful. Pray that you would not lose your sense of encouragement when you experience temporary failure. Ask God to bolster your ministry through prayer and objective assessments of your abilities, not subjective deceptions.

Prescribe

1 TIMOTHY 5:1-8

Do not rebuke an older man harshly, but exhort him as if he were your father. Treat younger men as brothers, [2] older women as mothers, and younger women as sisters, with absolute purity.

[3] Give proper recognition to those widows who are really in need. [4] But if a widow has children or grandchildren, these should learn first of all to put their religion into practice by caring for their own family and so repaying their parents and grandparents, for this is pleasing to God. [5] The widow who is really in need and left all alone puts her hope in God and continues night and day to pray and to ask God for help. [6] But the widow who lives for pleasure is dead even while she lives. [7] Give the people these instructions, so that no one may be open to blame. [8] Anyone who does not provide for their relatives, and especially for their own household, has denied the faith and is worse than an unbeliever.

The fifth chapter of 1 Timothy has much to say about family relationships within the Ephesian church. It was clearly important to Paul that the Ephesians be exemplary in their management of their family affairs. Perhaps these comments were delivered in response to observations he and Timothy had made of relationships in the church. Or perhaps they were just his take on issues at large in the secular culture of the day.

In 1 Timothy 5:1–6, Paul provides some general advice about being respectful toward young and old, male and female. He also discusses the treatment of widows, which evidently was an issue; this idea is developed further in 1 Timothy 5:9–16.

Then, in 1 Timothy 5:7, Paul emphasizes the weight of his advice by using a different word for command, *parangelle*, which the NIV translates as *"give these instructions."* It's a compound word from *para*, meaning "at the side of or nearby," and *aggelos*, which means "to bring tidings or messages." This is where we derive the term angel.

Parangelle was used in the military to indicate the passing on of a command in person. This would be an instruction given to someone in close proximity, as a superior officer might give to a subordinate. There was an expectation that the subordinate would both listen to the command and be obedient. The English word prescribe incorporates this same idea.

Paul's prescription (1 Timothy 5:1–2) includes not being harsh to our elders, being gracious to older women, and being more tolerant of our peers. He also stresses the importance of Timothy dealing with young women in purity.

We associate the word prescribe not with biblical counsel but with medicine. *Parangelle* paints the picture of an earnest health professional imparting sage advice to a patient with the hope and expectation that they might listen and adhere to it.

The importance of compliance is underlined by the second part of Paul's instruction in 1 Timothy 5:7: *"so that no one may be open to blame."* If a patient doesn't comply with medical advice and continues his high-risk behaviour, the physician cannot be blamed for the outcome.

So it is with family and personal relationships. If we adhere to Paul's directions, we aren't likely to suffer relational breakdown. This isn't a guarantee of a future without family problems, but it's a surefire way to ensure that the breakdown isn't a result of our own noncompliance.

Paul warns us as Christians in 1 Timothy 5:8 not to fall below the expectations placed on secular families in our personal relationships. To do so would deny our calling and dismiss the miracle of conversion that called us from our sleep to a life with Christ.

APPLICATION: PRESCRIBE

- When I think about perfectly neighbourly relationships, I often think of J.R.R. Tolkien's elves. There's something about being long-lived that made them deeply respectful of one another. When we find it difficult to comply with Paul's prescription, we might remember that as Christians we will have eternity to sort out our squabbles. In light of this truth, perhaps our hurts won't seem as devastating. Pray that in difficult relationships God would give you a sense of your eternity to shift your perspective.

- It takes time to see the wisdom of compliance. Think back on instances when you've done things God's way and not your own and appreciated the wisdom of His word. Thank God for His advice and for the way things turned out.
- Our behaviour toward one another is supposed to be irreproachable (1 Timothy 5:8), but sometimes we only reach the standards set by contemporary culture. Let us pray that we not fall below this. We need His strength to enable us to be beyond reproach.

Help

No widow may be put on the list of widows unless she is over sixty, has been faithful to her husband, [10] and is well known for her good deeds, such as bringing up children, showing hospitality, washing the feet of the Lord's people, helping those in trouble and devoting herself to all kinds of good deeds.

[11] As for younger widows, do not put them on such a list. For when their sensual desires overcome their dedication to Christ, they want to marry. [12] Thus they bring judgment on themselves, because they have broken their first pledge. [13] Besides, they get into the habit of being idle and going about from house to house. And not only do they become idlers, but also busybodies who talk nonsense, saying things they ought not to. 14 So I counsel younger widows to marry, to have children, to manage their homes and to give the enemy no opportunity for slander. [15] Some have in fact already turned away to follow Satan.

[16] If any woman who is a believer has widows in her care, she should continue to help them and not let the

church be burdened with them, so that the church can
help those widows who are really in need.

Christians are called to be compassionate toward the needs
of others. The silver commandment, *"Do to others as you
have them do to you"* (Luke 6:31), speaks to this calling. The good
Samaritan parable (Luke 10:25–37) was given to explain what
such compassion might look like.

Today's passage wasn't written to limit our compassion as
individuals, such teaching would be contrary to our faith. It was
given to the corporate body of the church so it would be wise in the
use of its resources when responding to compassionate requests.
The social and cultural climate of first-century life in Ephesus
meant that widows were often neglected and left destitute. They
weren't employable, as a rule, because of their lack of education
and were seen to have little to offer society outside the home.

Converting to Christianity should have changed a person's
perspective on how widows were treated. It's easy to see how the
sight of such impoverished and vulnerable women would have
tugged on a Christian's heartstrings.

How was the church to react to such a need? Paul provides
some practical advice. The goal of his advice is explained in 1
Timothy 5:16: *"so that the church can help those widows who are
really in need."*

The meaning of the word help in 1 Timothy 5:16 is complex.
It is from the Greek *eparkese*, although a more typical word for help
would have been *boetheo*, which was used when a person meant
to convey the type of help given in a person's time of distress. In

contrast, *eparkese* was derived from *epi* and *arkeo*, where *epi* serves as an intensifier, or superlative, to *arkeo*, which means "to assist or to meet one's needs/ be sufficient."

The idea in 1 Timothy 5:16 is that the church has plentiful resources not just to help widows sufficiently, but to go further than that. This wasn't just about survival; it was about restoring a person to life and enabling them to thrive.

To achieve this, a degree of corporate focus was required. This type of corporate focus didn't detract a Christian's primary calling to be compassionate; rather, it was about investing wisely in vulnerable people.

Paul highlighted some personal characteristics that could be used to identify genuine Christian widows (1 Timothy 5:9-10). He then commented on how to decide who might be more needy than others (1 Timothy 5:11-16).

Although his remarks related to the management of widows, some of his instructions are worth considering for solutions to other social problems facing our churches today. Sadly, there are many. We might consider groups on the fringes of our own churches who have made confessions of faith yet remain social outcasts, such as the homeless, drug addicts, divorcees, single parents, the mentally ill, refugees, the elderly, and the unemployed. All of these groups have social and financial needs.

Paul wrote that those that can help themselves should be given liberty to do it, lest the church encourage idleness. He also pointed out that families ought to be seen as another port of refuge for those in need of assistance. Lastly, he suggested that the church should support those who have no other source of support.

Passages like this one are challenging, for we so often read them as personal instructions. At the outset of this study, though, we acknowledged that there are three characters involved in 1 Timothy: Paul, Timothy, and the Ephesian church. This passage is directed at the church and instructs them on how to use their resources.

We might consider how we can help our modern equivalents of the Ephesian widows both individually and in our churches. If we revisit the parable of the good Samaritan and ask, against which groups do we hold the most prejudice? In other words, who are our Samaritans? In answering this, we come to understand who it is we are least likely to help.

APPLICATION: HELP

- Consider your own church and those on the fringes who might have needs. Pray about how you might raise awareness of their plight and whether there are ways in which you could help them beyond their basic financial needs.
- How does your church decide to whom they should extend compassionate support? Pray for those in leadership, that they may make wise decisions and follow some of the guidance suggested by Paul.
- Who are your Samaritans? Who do you perceive as the least likely to help others? Pray that you will have a more generous heart to your Samaritans. And where possible, seek to expand your growing heart by being generous.

Keep Pure

1 TIMOTHY 5:17–25

The elders who direct the affairs of the church well are worthy of double honor, especially those whose work is preaching and teaching. [18] For Scripture says, "Do not muzzle an ox while it is treading out the grain," and "The worker deserves his wages." [19] Do not entertain an accusation against an elder unless it is brought by two or three witnesses. [20] But those elders who are sinning you are to reprove before everyone, so that the others may take warning. [21] I charge you, in the sight of God and Christ Jesus and the elect angels, to keep these instructions without partiality, and to do nothing out of favoritism.

[22] Do not be hasty in the laying on of hands, and do not share in the sins of others. Keep yourself pure.

[23] Stop drinking only water, and use a little wine because of your stomach and your frequent illnesses.

[24] The sins of some are obvious, reaching the place of judgment ahead of them; the sins of others trail behind them. [25] In the same way, good deeds are obvious, and even those that are not obvious cannot remain hidden forever.

In these verses, Paul continues to give Timothy advice as to how to deal with corporate issues. He begins by discussing how to deal with good works and failings in the church's elders and finishes with the good works and sins of the congregation. In the middle, he leaves some personal comments for Timothy regarding how to make his ministry a success.

We could subtitle all of 1 Timothy 5 as "challenging conversations," since there are multiple opportunities for potential disputes. Timothy will have to be tactful yet firm in his dealings with the different groups if the church in Ephesus is to stay in tune with the gospel.

When churches manage such problems well, the issues never amount to more than a simmer. They don't boil over and in time they cool off. If, however, such issues are allowed to become heated, it's more difficult to manage the subsequent explosions.

The crux of Paul's advice to Timothy is to remain pure (1 Timothy 5:22). It comes at the end of the first series of difficult conversation topics (1 Timothy 5:17–22) and before the second set (1 Timothy 5:24–25).

Paul's instruction, *"Keep yourself pure"* (1 Timothy 5:22), would have been more closely translated in the original Greek as "Guard your freedom." The word used for guard/keep is *terei*, and the word use for free/pure is *hagnon*.

The value of Paul's advice to church leaders cannot be overstated, and yet it is often overlooked by congregations and ministry teams.

A pastor can grow tired, dusty, and hurt. There is a danger of becoming despondent, disillusioned, and unfocussed. For pastors to remain pure, to hold steadfast to the freedom they first experienced in Christ, they must constantly replenish themselves. In other words, they need to draw upon a ready store of Christ-like purity.

It's enormously difficult for church leaders to remain this pure. Of all the messages from 1 Timothy 5, we should acknowledge the challenges faced by those who lead us and spare a prayer that they would be given the grace and encouragement they need to remain pure.

I'm not sure what the twenty-first century equivalent of a little wine might be in our church leaders, but Paul suggested that such eccentricities should be permitted if they help to calm people's anxieties. Perhaps one of the uncomfortable but caring conversations we need with our pastors is to find out what their equivalents of a little wine might be.

APPLICATION: KEEP PURE

- Pray for your church leaders, that they would retain a generous measure of the naivety they had when they first believed. Ask God to protect them from the politics of the church so they may continue to preach the gospel with vibrancy.
- Thank God for the willingness of church leaders to continue to preach the gospel in our secular world and to run the gauntlet of leading without fear of persecution.

• Take a moment to consider how we maintain our purity, our naivety, in Christ. What stops you from becoming discouraged? What sips of wine might you need to take to help settle your nerves and allow your soul to keep free in Christ?

Coming to understand the other person, and yourself, more deeply doesn't mean that differences will disappear or that you won't have to solve real problems and make real choices. It doesn't mean that all views are equally valid or that its wrong to have strongly held beliefs. It will, however, help you evaluate whether your strong views make sense in light of new information and different interpretations, and it will help you help others to appreciate the power of those views.[12]

—Douglas Stone, Bruce Patton, and Sheila Heen

12 Douglas Stone, Bruce Patton, and Sheila Heen, *Difficult Conversations* (New York, NY: Penguin Books, 2010), 43.

Great Gain

1 TIMOTHY 6:1–10

All who are under the yoke of slavery should consider their masters worthy of full respect, so that God's name and our teaching may not be slandered. [2] Those who have believing masters should not show them disrespect just because they are fellow believers. Instead, they should serve them even better because their masters are dear to them as fellow believers and are devoted to the welfare of their slaves.

These are the things you are to teach and insist on. [3] If anyone teaches otherwise and does not agree to the sound instruction of our Lord Jesus Christ and to godly teaching, [4] they are conceited and understand nothing. They have an unhealthy interest in controversies and quarrels about words that result in envy, strife, malicious talk, evil suspicions [5] and constant friction between people of corrupt mind, who have been robbed of the truth and who think that godliness is a means to financial gain.

[6] But godliness with contentment is great gain. [7] For we brought nothing into the world, and we can take nothing out of it. [8] But if we have food and clothing, we

will be content with that. [9] Those who want to get rich fall into temptation and a trap and into many foolish and harmful desires that plunge people into ruin and destruction. [10] For the love of money is a root of all kinds of evil. Some people, eager for money, have wandered from the faith and pierced themselves with many griefs.

1 Timothy 6 begins with Paul providing Timothy with instructions on how to hold even more difficult conversations. He wrote of two further scenarios. In each case, although Paul handed his teaching to Timothy, the lessons were to be passed on to the church.

Paul addressed both the issue of Christian slaves under Christian masters and the prosperity gospel.

I don't wish to diminish the appalling nature of slavery, or the abuses committed under the guise of segregation or hurt from discrimination, yet it's more likely today to find Christians working under the direction of a Christian supervisor than it is to encounter a slave-master relationship.

We might therefore take notice of Paul's advice. Should we find ourselves working for a Christian, we might consider ways to ensure that we don't cause them to stumble. If it were possible, we might consider how to elevate their work performance through our own dedication.

From 1 Timothy 6:3–10, Paul addresses financial concerns. It would appear that the prosperity gospel, the promise of wealth through Christianity, had already started to spread.

Sadly, making money from religious activities began long before the first century. Philosophers of the ancient world already had a reputation for promising the world to those who adhered to their perspectives. Unfortunately, the same message was voiced by some Christians, and it seems similar messages were being preached in Ephesus.

In these verses, Paul crystallizes his own thoughts on the topic. Having established that the hunger for financial gain is responsible for much of the torment in the church, he writes that *"godliness with contentment is great gain"* (1 Timothy 6:6).

When writing about gain, Paul didn't choose to use the usual Greek word for profit, *ophelos*. Instead he uses the word *porismon*, which speaks to the method of obtaining benefit, not just the benefit on its own. Thus we understand that not only does godliness bestow contentment, but it also trains contentment or maturity in its practitioner.

The gain, or maturity, mentioned in 1 Timothy 6:6 is the freedom from envy, strife, malicious talk, evil suspicions, and constant friction. As mature Christians, we wish to be free of these traits, just as Paul implored Timothy to free the Ephesians from them. The absence of such would be living proof of our gain in Christian maturity—and it would be a great gain, a gain that Paul insists has a method.

It is possible to be godly, or righteous, but far from Christ just as Paul was in his life as a Pharisee. It is also possible to be godly with resentment, doing what we know to be right but without any spiritual investment. This was a problem for the rich young ruler in Matthew 19:16–26. He was very godly, but he couldn't respond when Jesus asked for a sign of his spiritual maturity.

Our training, though, is be godly with contentment, godly with spiritual accord not discord.

When we feel conflicted and lacking in contentment, Paul's words can be helpful, especially if our conflict involves financial concerns. At those times, remember that true gain is achieved through sticking with godliness with spiritual accord.

APPLICATION: GREAT GAIN

- What do you want? As Christians, we hope and pray for maturity in Christ. That would be a great gain. Paul says that this comes through godliness with contentment, so take a moment to be content with God.

- How is contentment different from peace? Contentment means being refreshed, prepared, and ready. A contented individual is still motivated. Pray that some of the energy from being content in Christ would impact your actions today.

- In 1 Timothy 6:6, Paul uses the words *mega porismos*, meaning "great gain." Mega is a word we have adopted into English. It's also become a colloquialism for anything that's considered amazing. Being in Christ as a Christian is an amazing gain. It should put into perspective our conflicts, including financial ones. Pray for a fresh sense of your mega gain in Christ.

The shocked question of the disciples "Who then can be saved?" seems to indicate that they regarded the case of the rich young man not as in any way exceptional, but as typical. For they do not ask: "Which rich man?" but quite generally, "Who then can be saved?" For every man, even the disciples themselves, belongs to those rich ones for whom it is so difficult to enter the kingdom of heaven. The answer Jesus gives showed the disciples that they had understood him well. Salvation through following Jesus is not something we men can achieve for ourselves—but with God all things are possible.[13]

---

13 Dietrich Bonhoeffer, *The Cost of Discipleship* (New York, NY: Touchstone, 1995), 85.

Take Hold

1 TIMOTHY 6:11–21

But you, man of God, flee from all this, and pursue righteousness, godliness, faith, love, endurance and gentleness. [12] Fight the good fight of the faith. Take hold of the eternal life to which you were called when you made your good confession in the presence of many witnesses. [13] In the sight of God, who gives life to everything, and of Christ Jesus, who while testifying before Pontius Pilate made the good confession, I charge you [14] to keep this command without spot or blame until the appearing of our Lord Jesus Christ, [15] which God will bring about in his own time—God, the blessed and only Ruler, the King of kings and Lord of lords, [16] who alone is immortal and who lives in unapproachable light, whom no one has seen or can see. To him be honor and might forever. Amen.

[17] Command those who are rich in this present world not to be arrogant nor to put their hope in wealth, which is so uncertain, but to put their hope in God, who richly provides us with everything for our enjoyment. [18] Command them to do good, to be rich in good deeds, and to be generous and willing to share.

[19] In this way they will lay up treasure for themselves as a firm foundation for the coming age, so that they may take hold of the life that is truly life.

[20] Timothy, guard what has been entrusted to your care. Turn away from godless chatter and the opposing ideas of what is falsely called knowledge, [21] which some have professed and in so doing have departed from the faith.

Grace be with you all.

P aul finishes his letter with four different endings, each briefer than the preceding one, each having a different emphasis. But they all have the same focus: Paul expressing his regard for Timothy.

At the end of this first goodbye (1 Timothy 6:11–16), Paul was moved to give thanks in a doxology. In doing so, he expressed not just his gratitude for God but also how much Timothy meant to him. Paul was moved to praise God as he imagined the tasks Timothy faced, the progress his disciple had made, and the adventures they'd had together.

The letter could have ended here. It would have been fitting and left Timothy on a high as he read Paul's words, moved by Paul's doxology and the strength of his inspiring recap.

Paul continued, though, with a second farewell (1 Timothy 6:17–19). These verses are almost an afterthought to his comments in 1 Timothy 6:1–10 concerning wealth. Those earlier verses spoke to the perils of wealth and may have led wealthier church members to have felt anxious of their salvation. Here, however,

Paul gives Timothy some tips for those left who feel insecure in their roles due to money, advising them to may take hold of life and salvation.

In yet a third ending (1 Timothy 6:20–21), he bid Timothy to guard well the gospel which had been entrusted to him. It was a reminder to hold onto the simplicity of the gospel with a steadfastness not readily shaken by earthly distractions. Paul's insistence of this was something he emphasized in his own ministry, too. Sound doctrine was important in order to stress the simplicity of the gospel, but it also could combat false teachings that tried to add to the self-sufficiency of Christ's work.

Finally, Paul relayed a fourth goodbye, a characteristic reflection on the grace of God. With this closing gesture, he signed off to his son in the faith.

Through these four endings, it seems as though Paul is moving through Timothy's house at the end of a social gathering. He begins his farewell in the conservatory, off the kitchen. He begins with effusive words, a message of hope and reinstatement. It's a goodbye that seems to say, "Great to see you. Better let you crack on. Fantastic work. You're a super guy. You'll do great."

Then, as he makes his way to the figurative hall and front door, he remembers there was something he forgot to add. Something important! He wants to encourage others to hold on, just as he wants Timothy to hold on. This is his second goodbye.

When Paul arrives at the front door and is just about to leave, he gives another parting message, telling Timothy to keep the message safe, take care of his family, and look after those entrusted to him. Then he goes.

But as he makes his way from Timothy's house, he turns one last time. He makes eye contact with his son in the faith and waves. It's a virtual hug for someone so special to him, a virtual acknowledgement of what has passed between them as disciple and mentor, father figure and son, brothers in Christ.

What ties these four endings together is the concept of holding on. Paul implored Timothy to take hold of eternal life and to encourage the wealthy to do likewise, to hold onto the truth of the gospel and the grace which binds us all.

The word Paul uses for "take hold" in 1 Timothy 6:12 is *epilabou*, from *epi* (in the Greek, "upon") and *lambano* ("to take hold"). By choosing *epilabou*, Paul is saying that it's not enough for Timothy to simply hold onto his salvation. He has to wrestle and grapple with eternal life so that it doesn't escape. The implication is that if we grip too lightly, if we don't take hold of the truth of our salvation securely, we could lose it. It might be more theologically correct to say that we might become deceived through our lack of commitment to the simplicity of the gospel and begin to follow a wrong path. This path, in time, could lead us astray.

In this, we might remember Mr. Worldly-Wiseman from *The Pilgrim's Progress*. He spoke so eloquently that he put Christian off his path.[14]

To counter this possibility, Paul charged Timothy to flee from earthly distractions and fasten onto his salvation.

---

14 Bunyan, *The Pilgrim's Progress*, 13–17.

APPLICATION: TAKE HOLD

- There is an emphasis in these closing verses of grasping tightly to the life, gospel, brotherhood, and grace we have been given through Christ. Take a moment to thank God for each of these and appreciate the joy that each instills.
- How secure is your hold? What do you cling to when you doubt God's purposes for your life? Thank God for the simplicity of the gospel and the generosity of His grace.
- Could you pray for a tighter hold, a stronger grip? Pray that Paul's closing words to Timothy would be an encouragement that you would remain fixed to the simplicity of His message and firm in your rejection of false teaching.

Reflections

1 TIMOTHY

Watch your life and doctrine closely. Persevere in them, because if you do, you will save both yourself and your hearers. (1 Timothy 4:16)

In this first installment of the pastoral letters from Paul to Timothy, Paul means for Timothy to cultivate a godly environment for Christianity to flourish in Ephesus. He is looking to Timothy to prune the parts of the Ephesian acreage that had become unruly and to feed where the growth looked promising. This growth, whether personal or corporate, was complex, pushing forward in some directions while cutting back in others.

It is an interesting perspective to consider that a church, as a corporate body, has a personality—and its personality traits can change over time.

According to Jesus in the first letter to the churches in Asia, the Ephesian church had many promising traits (Revelation 2:2–6). They had persevered. They had been intolerant of false apostles and wickedness. They had endured hardships and not grown weary. Jesus warned them though not to forget their first love, the emotion they had felt when they first believed. Pruning was still required or the church's focus on Christ would become overshadowed, overgrown, and hidden.

It seems to me this was also part of Paul's message for the Ephesians via Timothy. He left instructions for them to have a pure heart, keep pure, and maintain a clear, unspoilt perspective of Christ, both personally and corporately. The church's personality, after all, is a reflection of its parts. It is a mosaic of all our personalities, which should in turn be reflective of Christ.

On an individual level, I think we know that our personalities change over time, but we either don't give it much thought or we tend to deny that we change. We consider ourselves to be set in our ways.

Aging does lead to aching joints and poor mobility, but our personalities don't need to become equally inflexible with time. Rather, we read our Bibles so we can better understand Him and align ourselves accordingly. In understanding Him, we come to know ourselves better. In the process, we acknowledge where we have work to do.

Although this introspection is important and relevant to the corporate personality of the church, by reflecting on 1 Timothy I can also see how important pastoral personality is. I became more aware of the difficulties that pastors like Timothy have to face.

Just as the distractions haven't changed much in two thousand years, the pressures on pastors have not reduced. Such pressures could loosen their grip on the simplicity of the gospel.

The danger is, as it was for Timothy and the Ephesians, that if the grip doesn't hold false teaching can occur, disillusionment can creep in, and the church can suffer. It could become overgrown with weeds, choking out growth.

In reflecting on these challenges for those who lead us, rather than praying for personal change and growth, I found myself thinking of those who have been instrumental in my faith, those I know who have kept a pure heart, maintained a sound doctrine, and whose hold on the gospel is secure.

With this perspective, 1 Timothy becomes a pastoral letter again as it prompts prayers for pastors past and present, near and far, young and old. My prayer is that they would remain aligned to the simplicity of the gospel and remain free from the distractions of church politics.

In our leaders we should look for some of the eagerness that comes from a vibrant faith. We should wish to be led by those who have a pure heart and a strong grip on eternal life and sound doctrine.

I suspect this isn't easy for ministers to maintain. Even Timothy needed support. Our prayers for steadfastness in the gospel, and pursuit of eternal life and grace, will be beneficial. But so too will be the occasional gracious deed or gift.

Introduction

When we finish a book like 1 Timothy that is the first in a series, we seldom press on to read the second book as we might with a collection of novels. Instead we stop after the first installment and choose next to read a book of the Bible from another series. This has been my experience when reading 1 and 2 Timothy. I've read them at widely separated times, often years apart and in different churches or small groups.

It's also true, given the timespan that passed between the writing of these letters, that Paul may have been less acquainted with what he wrote in 1 Timothy when he wrote 2 Timothy. I doubt he had a copy his first letter on hand when he composed the second. In that sense, we have an advantage, for we can more readily spot similarities and differences between them.

Paul's second letter to Timothy was written in AD 66–68, five or six years after his first. In contrast to 1 Timothy, 2 Timothy was not written from a place of freedom. It wasn't written from the supportive environment of the church of Philippi. Instead 2 Timothy was penned from a cold prison in Rome, perhaps even the notorious Mamertine prison from which few were set free.

Unlike the changes which had beset Paul, Timothy's life was similar. He was still in Ephesus and his ministry there continued. We will see that in 2 Timothy there are fewer instructions for Timothy to pass on. There are also fewer commands to realign the Ephesians. Perhaps this change in emphasis was a reflection of the successes Timothy had enjoyed from following the directions found in 1 Timothy.

Rather than a letter of corporate, congregational advice to a young minister, 2 Timothy is a more personal letter. It seeks to build Timothy's heart. Paul's mission may be the same, to build the church, but his emphasis here is to build up Timothy to be better equipped to build the church. Different play, same goal.

Although Paul's emphasis was different, the shift from corporate instruction manual to personal correspondence seems fitting. It seems particularly appropriate in light of how 1 Timothy closed. We glimpsed something of the closeness that comes from working with someone for thirty to forty years.

Paul and Timothy weren't simply colleagues. Their relationship was a teacher-pupil, tutor-disciple, father-son. There was a dependency between them, and no doubt also respect and honesty. There was also the common bond of believing in Christ, which drew them closer to each other through their shared vision and goals.

In having just finished 1 Timothy, where we tasted this familiarity between the two, we are fortunate to be able to appreciate even more the strength of sentiment in Paul's language in 2 Timothy.

Paul's impassioned writing in this second letter might also reflect his own position. Although his ability to remain calm was impressive, no doubt reflecting his colossal confidence in God, he must have sensed that his release was unlikely.

At this desperate time, Paul reached deep into his heart to write this last letter, addressed to the person who perhaps knew him most and with whom he had shared so much.

As we transition from 1 Timothy to 2 Timothy, it is worth pausing. Few experience what Paul and Timothy lived through. Ours is a post-Christian world, not pre-Christian like the world these men lived in. They had the joy of seeing people brought to life, lifted from despair, elevated from their purposeless drifting, and given hope.

Some evangelists today have similar experiences, but the ordeals Paul and Timothy endured were original to them. There had been no forerunners, no one who could have predicted their success. There hadn't been any prior Christian revivals. From a religious perspective, they were living in a brave new world. In that unprecedented environment they worked as a team to listen and act as God directed them.

Perhaps some today can relate to their closeness. They were like soldiers serving together. However, my sense is that the partnership between Paul and Timothy was rare—not unique, but infrequent.

When we read 2 Timothy, we ought to remember all of these emotions Paul must have been writing from. Our goal is to seek out what Paul was burning to pass on to Timothy. What were the final lessons he wished to communicate? How would he build up his son to take on his mantle, his leadership role? These instructions will be worth learning for ourselves, so we can pass them on to others.

Identity

2 TIMOTHY 1:1–2

Paul, an apostle of Christ Jesus by the will of God, in
keeping with the promise of life that is in Christ Jesus,
[2] To Timothy, my dear son: Grace, mercy and peace
from God the Father and Christ Jesus our Lord.

If there was a moment when we might expect people to
reconsider their identity, it would be when they're in jail. In
such confined and isolated circumstances, the mind wanders.

At a time when we might expect Paul to question who he
was, we find him doubling down on the traits that led to his arrest.
Rather than renouncing the identity that had subjugated him to a
dark, damp, cold dungeon, Paul restated who, what, and why he was.

Paul knew who he was. He was no longer Saul. Instead
he was Paul, a changed man called by Christ not to persecute
the Christian church but to help build it. He had no alternative
identity, no one else he could become. He knew who God had
made him to be. He couldn't renounce God, for it would have
been tantamount to renouncing himself. Paul appreciated the
truth of Psalm 139:13–14 and saw no alternative beyond what
God had called him to become.

Paul knew what he was. He had heard Christ's voice call him (Acts 9). He was an apostle of Christ Jesus. As an *apostolos*, Paul was a sent one, sent directly by Christ. The title conferred additional authority in the ancient church since Paul and the remaining disciples were the only ones on whom it had been bestowed. It was given in recognition of their unique anointing by Christ to the task of seeking the lost under the great commission (Matthew 28:18–20).

Paul knew why he was—why he was no longer Saul, why he had become an apostle. The reason was consistent with the promise of Christ to bring life. When Saul converted to Paul, he found life (2 Timothy 1:1, John 10:10). Christ also promised to deliver a life full of potential.

He was Paul, not Saul, because Christ had fulfilled these promises.

It seems poignant to read of Paul being given life to the full even when confined to his prison cell. His hope was sustained by the depth and breadth of his memories, which included his poignant calling. Such was his clarity that Paul was still able to talk of a full life despite his circumstances.

I hope we never find ourselves in Paul's predicament, persecuted or imprisoned for our faith. It is more likely we will experience subtle pressure to conform to our secular culture. Under such conditions, there will be times when our identities in Christ will be awkward to maintain.

There is reassurance in this book's opening statement and a realism, a concrete quality, that is difficult to deny. By making it personal, putting our name into this verse reminds us that God

Identity: 2 Timothy 1:1-2

Himself has given each of us a unique identity which is fully realized by our relationship with Him through Christ. This was so important to Paul that we should name it for ourselves, just like he did.

APPLICATION: IDENTITY

- Take a moment to recognize your own identity in Christ. If it's helpful, use 2 Timothy 1:1 as a guide, making a small modification to reflect the fact we are not apostles but disciples. Read it like this: "(Your name), a disciple of Christ Jesus by the will of God, in keeping with the promise of life that is in Christ Jesus…"

- Part of our identity in Christ is bound to our receiving of the Holy Spirit, a gift Paul refers to as an anointing (2 Corinthians 1:21–22). Our anointing doesn't confer messianic status, but it does reflect the new identity we received when we were born again. Thank God that you are anointed, protected and sealed with His Holy Spirit.

- By the grace of God, Paul was no longer Saul. Give thanks for Paul's life and his commitment to the gospel. Remember in your prayers all the Paul-like figures who have mentored you. Remember those who, being secure in their calling, have embodied their new identities in Christ.

He says, "I am come that they might have life, and that they might have it more abundantly." And when you have had that life from him, even as you face death, you will be able to say with this mighty apostle, "To me to live is Christ, and to die is gain", because it means "to be with Christ; which is far better" (Philippians 1:21 and 23).[15]

---

15 D. Martyn Lloyd-Jones, *I Am Not Ashamed: Advice to Timothy* (Grand Rapids, MI: Baker Books, 1986), 88.

Self-Discipline

2 TIMOTHY 1:3-10

I thank God, whom I serve, as my ancestors did, with a clear conscience, as night and day I constantly remember you in my prayers. [4] Recalling your tears, I long to see you, so that I may be filled with joy. [5] I am reminded of your sincere faith, which first lived in your grandmother Lois and in your mother Eunice and, I am persuaded, now lives in you also.

[6] For this reason I remind you to fan into flame the gift of God, which is in you through the laying on of my hands. [7] For the Spirit God gave us does not make us timid, but gives us power, love and self-discipline. [8] So do not be ashamed of the testimony about our Lord or of me his prisoner. Rather, join with me in suffering for the gospel, by the power of God. [9] He has saved us and called us to a holy life—not because of anything we have done but because of his own purpose and grace. This grace was given us in Christ Jesus before the beginning of time, [10] but it has now been revealed through the appearing of our Savior, Christ Jesus, who has destroyed death and has brought life and immortality to light through the gospel.

Resonance is what happens when a force creates a larger than expected response in an object. It is predicted by the observation that all matter vibrates invisibly. If an external force is set at a particular frequency, the same natural oscillating frequency of the object, the object can resonate in response to the force.

Let's consider the example of a child on a swing. The swing has a natural frequency that's determined by the length of the rope and the speed of the swing. If the child applies a small force by moving their legs, and if they move in time with the natural frequency of the swing, then even this small force can keep the child in constant motion.

There is something of a resonance interaction between Paul and Timothy. For half of Timothy's life, Paul was the external influence, gently pushing Timothy, nurturing his natural frequency to enable him to achieve greater things for God than he might have done on his own.

I suspect that the relationship was reciprocal. Paul benefitted from having the encouragement of his disciple (2 Timothy 1:4). Timothy pushed Paul to be more productive than he might otherwise have been.

Given the closeness of their relationship, it seems almost natural for Paul, having called out his own identity, to go on and to speak of Timothy's. Paul called out his disciple's sincere faith, which was established by his grandmother and mother. Paul reminded him of his anointing for ministry through the laying on of hands. Paul emphasized that Timothy had the Holy Spirit, which enables through the gifts of strength, grace, and self-discipline.

Paul was gently pushing Timothy to get him moving.

Self-Discipline: 2 Timothy 1:3-10

There may be some truth in the observation that Paul and Timothy had a potentiating effect on each other's lives. They would have been the first to admit that any influence they had on each other paled when compared to the effect Jesus had on their lives. Christ provides the biggest push on our swings, moving us into a relationship with Him so we can resonate in sympathy with His natural frequency.

As Christians, we differ from the secular world by our acceptance that others might have a role to guide our lives. It's an anathema to many that someone other than themselves may guide their identity.

In contrast, by choosing to follow God, the Christian sets off on a path which, if followed to Christian maturity, causes one to bring glory to God and diminish self. The Christian seeks to resonate with what God has bestowed on us, fulfilling His vision for our lives. Our lives will be enriched and lived abundantly according to His promises when we chose to live for Him and not ourselves.

Paul in these introductory verses wrote of his own commitment to this path and proceeded to remind Timothy that he too was called to pursue this same path. In order to stay on the path, Timothy would need self-discipline (2 Timothy 1:7). It is self-discipline that reminds us as Christians who we live for, who we seek to follow, whose desires we wish to fulfill, and who must increase and who should diminish (John 3:30).

Self-discipline is not selfish discipline. It's a significant gift of the Spirit (2 Timothy 1:7). Self-discipline is translated from the Greek *sophronismos*, meaning a sound or saved mind. The Holy

Spirit helps to settle our anxieties and wandering ideas, enabling us to embrace disciplined thoughts and avoid excessive self-indulgence.

Rather than dwelling on anxieties and fears, Paul reminded Timothy that he had been given the Holy Spirit to help focus his thoughts and discipline his mind. Paul focussed Timothy's thoughts away from any selfish ideas his disciple may have been entertaining. Paul's goal was to set Timothy back into his natural frequency, so he could be most productive.

Being reminded of our past Christian experiences can be useful in terms of reenergizing our commitment, gently pushing us back into a rhythm of sound thought about ourselves, our roles, and our calling.

If the preceding verses weren't enough encouragement, Paul went on in 2 Timothy 1:9–10 to nudge Timothy some more by using the gospel. Provided there was a ripple of belief in Timothy's faith, Jesus's life, death, and resurrection would surely resonate with it, serving to swing Timothy into a committed walk along the path to Christian maturity.

APPLICATION: SELF-DISCIPLINE

- Consider the gift of the Holy Spirit. Remind yourself of His gifts of power, love, and self-discipline. Allow your thoughts to turn to gratitude.
- We don't often thank God for marshalling our thoughts and bringing discipline to our ideas and

anxieties. Take a moment to pray for soundness of thought so your thoughts may conform to His.

• Thank Him for the ways in which He brings resonance into your life to enable you to live abundantly for Him.

Man needs to be saved. He will never have peace and rest, he will never be able to say, as he faces life at its worst, "nevertheless I am not ashamed" until he has been delivered from himself, delivered from the thraldom of circumstances, from the world, the flesh, the devil, delivered by God, to God, for God, and finds his rest and peace in the arms of God.[16]

---

16 Ibid.

Know

And of this gospel I was appointed a herald and an apostle and a teacher. [12] That is why I am suffering as I am. Yet this is no cause for shame, because I know whom I have believed, and am convinced that he is able to guard what I have entrusted to him until that day.

[13] What you heard from me, keep as the pattern of sound teaching, with faith and love in Christ Jesus. [14] Guard the good deposit that was entrusted to you— guard it with the help of the Holy Spirit who lives in us.

[15] You know that everyone in the province of Asia has deserted me, including Phygelus and Hermogenes.

[16] May the Lord show mercy to the household of Onesiphorus, because he often refreshed me and was not ashamed of my chains. [17] On the contrary, when he was in Rome, he searched hard for me until he found me. [18] May the Lord grant that he will find mercy from the Lord on that day! You know very well in how many ways he helped me in Ephesus.

In the first few verses of 2 Timothy, Paul explained his identity. He called out the identity Timothy had in Christ and distilled the gospel. In doing this, Paul reminded Timothy of God's gracious plan for salvation. He stressed the reality of Christ's appearing, retold Jesus's death, and declared the truth of the resurrection.

At the conclusion of this distillation, Paul declared that he knew the identity of Christ: *"I know whom I have believed"* (2 Timothy 1:12).

Knowing Christ intimately, personally, and completely resonated so soundly with Paul that he couldn't be ashamed. Like a parent with their child, a groom with his bride, a mountaineer with their mountain, shame cannot be on the agenda. It would be unthinkable, unnatural, and inappropriate.

The Greek word Paul used for "know" was *eido*, which conveys more than simply seeing and acknowledging. It expresses an understanding and a recognition, a familiarity and trust with something or someone. We can know an acquaintance, but we might say that we truly *eido* our siblings, whom we have lived with.

This word speaks to an additional degree of understanding. This further element of knowledge that Paul expresses isn't intellectual knowledge; if it were, Paul might be guilty of Gnosticism.[17] The additional component expressed in *eido* is trust, dependency, reliability. So sure was Paul of Christ's love that he knew Jesus to be worthy of his devotion. For Paul, Christ was the mountain on his horizon; forever present, forever unchanging. Christ was no cold mountain, though, but a gracious savour who had rescued Paul.

It would be remiss not to point out that life wasn't going well for Paul at the time he wrote this letter. Christ didn't appear

---

17 The Gnostics were an early branch of Christianity that stresses a secret knowledge, or *gnosis*, would could provide a means of achieving salvation.

to be helping him escape from prison, win over new converts, or spread the gospel. Quite the opposite was occurring. Paul was imprisoned on death row, abandoned by other Christians who had become shy and intimidated by his imprisonment.

How can we understand the difference between the faith of Paul, and Onesiphorus versus Phygelus, and Hermogenes?

For a Christian, there are really only two days of spiritual significance: *this day* and *that day*.

That day, which Paul refers to in 2 Timothy 1:18, is the day when we meet Jesus for the second time—when He returns and we enter heaven, when we rely on the birth, death, and resurrection of Christ to join Him and the Father. It's the beginning of our new life in heaven on the new earth in all its glory.

This day is when day we encounter the resurrected Jesus for the first time. It's the moment Saul became Paul, when he was born again. Until then, Saul couldn't conceive of Christ as the Messiah. He couldn't accept the miracles, teachings, or death of Christ, or even the fulfillment of scripture. Only meeting with the resurrected Jesus changed Paul's knowledge of the man from Jesus son of Joseph to Jesus the anointed one.

Once Jesus was revealed, appearing from behind the clouds of Saul's pride, there could be no return. Revelation knowledge, *eido*, had come to Paul and it was impossible for him to deny the presence of the mountain that was Christ.

This day gave Paul the confidence, the trust, to persevere with Christianity despite his present circumstances. It's the day when Jesus was revealed.

Know: 2 Timothy 1:11-18

Timothy didn't appear have the same momentous conversion that Paul experienced. If Timothy had, Paul would have reminded his disciple of it. Timothy's experience was probably much like many of ours. We have read, listened, been taught, and become convinced that the gospel is true. We have prayed to receive Christ and His Holy Spirit into our lives. We believe because something in the gospel appeals to our souls.

Paul reminded Timothy that he had entrusted his life to Christ—his eternal life, not just the temporary life in prison (2 Timothy 1:12). For Paul, this was the sound teaching, the critical perspective, the pivotal point, the cornerstone of faith. This perspective was not to be lost, diluted, or forgotten (2 Timothy 1:13).

It is a sobering teaching. Unless we give over our eternal lives to Christ, we won't experience the depth of belief that Paul exhibited. In other words, we will lose perspective if we don't come to understand that we have a soul. Our Christianity will be a shallow commitment.

Such shallow commitments are readily shaken if they aren't based on genuine resurrection experiences of *this day*. In contrast, when we experience the call of Christ to eternal life there is no returning to the fishing nets, the tax books, or pride of self-fulfillment.

When we respond to *this day*, we respond to the eternal perspective that God placed in our hearts (Ecclesiastes 3:11). We acknowledge that which is highest in ourselves, that which makes us uniquely human.

This is the pattern of teaching which Paul declares as "sound." It is to be guarded so as to remain intact. Unless we experience the

93

resurrected Christ, unless we embrace the eternal perspective, we will not ascribe to this sound teaching, nor will we know Christ as Paul did. Knowing Him is more that a tipping of our heads; it is acknowledging that which we have always known to be true.

APPLICATION: KNOW

- Experiencing the resurrected Christ, knowing Him the *eido* way, can take many forms. It may be in a dramatic sense, as it was for Paul, or it could come through hearing the gospel or the works of others. Think about how you have encountered Christ and thank God for those experiences.
- Having an encounter with the resurrected Christ was important to Paul. It changed his life. Think back to your own conversion. Thank God for that time and those who helped to bring it about.
- Knowing Christ doesn't end at conversion. We spend our lives strengthening our knowledge, learning to rely on Him more and grow in our trust. We aspire to be like Paul in his devotion to see Christ as a mountain, solid and dependable—not just for our present lives, but for the lives to come. Let this thought lead you in prayer to seek Him more readily, and rely on him more dependably.

This is, I repeat, what makes man man—that over and above his bodily animal part there is this other part, unseen and intangible but of which we are all aware. A man cannot think of himself as going out of existence. You may think or say that when you die it is the end, but you cannot believe that, or even imagine it, because there is something about us that suggests we are immortal, that man was not made to die. We know that there is this other element in us which is imperishable. And this is the essence of the biblical teaching. Here the apostle says, "I am as I am, and I am able to say 'nevertheless' because I know my soul is safe. Let them do what they like to my body, they cannot touch my soul," he says. It is the fact that he knows he has got a soul that really gives him the confidence that he shows here.[18]

---

18 Lloyd-Jones, *I Am Not Ashamed*, 80.

Reflect

You then, my son, be strong in the grace that is in Christ Jesus. [2] And the things you have heard me say in the presence of many witnesses entrust to reliable people who will also be qualified to teach others. [3] Join with me in suffering, like a good soldier of Christ Jesus. [4] No one serving as a soldier gets entangled in civilian affairs, but rather tries to please his commanding officer. [5] Similarly, anyone who competes as an athlete does not receive the victor's crown except by competing according to the rules. [6] The hardworking farmer should be the first to receive a share of the crops. [7] Reflect on what I am saying, for the Lord will give you insight into all this.

[8] Remember Jesus Christ, raised from the dead, descended from David. This is my gospel, [9] for which I am suffering even to the point of being chained like a criminal. But God's word is not chained. [10] Therefore I endure everything for the sake of the elect, that they too may obtain the salvation that is in Christ Jesus, with eternal glory.

[11] Here is a trustworthy saying: If we died with him, we will also live with him; [12] if we endure, we

will also reign with him. If we disown him, he will also disown us; [13] if we are faithless, he remains faithful, for he cannot disown himself.

Paul transitions from writing of Jesus the man mountain, who was a constant presence, to presenting Timothy with three aspirational pictures of what a person's life looks like when lived with the mountain in view.

He writes of a soldier, an athlete, and a farmer, each epitomized by their own strength of character. The soldier fulfills his duties come hell and high water. The athlete endures despite opposition and physical challenges. The farmer must pit himself against the rigors of nature with its capriciousness and unforgiving temperament. For all three, there can be no surrender, no prize in conceding. Resignation is not in their character.

Paul suggests to Timothy that he consider these examples. He tells Timothy to reflect on them, using the Greek word *noei*, which can be translated as "think carefully." This word gives rise to the English colloquialism "to use your *nous*," which means to use your mind or think about what you're doing. Paul is encouraging his disciple to spend time pondering these examples. We might say that Paul is telling Timothy to deliberate intentionally on them, even meditate on them.

Each of the examples has a double edge.

Yes, the soldier demonstrates strength. He also manifests focus. Paul says that we shouldn't become entangled in church politics or secular affairs. Instead we should focus on the gospel, keeping the mission on mission.

The athlete is the personification of physical strength, yet he must also stay on track. He cannot deviate from the rules of the game. He must be obedient to the referee and laws of the competition. The message to the Christian is that they must remember who they worship, who is the centre of their attention, whose team they're on. We don't fight on our own or according to our own rules or wants. Rather we are on His team, under His management. We march under His banner.

A farmer is a symbol of perseverance against the natural world. Farmers strive to survive despite weather, poor soil, or pestilence. They live by faith that their endeavours will bear a reward. They are the embodiment of strong character, for theirs is a life of rigorous pursuit to provide the bare essentials. Paul encourages Timothy, assuring him that his labour will not go unrewarded. The hardworking Christian plants and nourishes in good faith the seeds which have been given to him. And when the time comes, an eschatological reward will be granted in heaven.

By thinking intentionally on these examples, Paul tells Timothy that God will provide further insight into their applicability to Timothy's situation.

He then finishes this part of the letter with another view of the mountain of Christ: the magnificent gospel. He reminds Timothy of Jesus's humanity and divinity, including His earthy heritage from David and His heavenly pedigree which defeats death.

This was like a breath to Paul, so deeply did he believe it to be true. This eloquent synopsis leads him into a short poem, a series of verses that finish with the emphatic conclusion that God cannot disown Himself. The mountain cannot become a pebble. It cannot dissolve from our view. It is faithful and persists.

Whether for the strong soldier, the endurance athlete, or the resilient farmer, the mountain remains steady on their horizon, providing sustenance for their labour. If Timothy needed this encouragement, these examples would help him refocus his game and to reimagine his reward.

I suspect we need to be reminded of the same. If Timothy working away in Ephesus needed to hear these sobering words from his father in the faith, we should pay attention too. God the Father and Jesus His Son remain on our horizons too. Perhaps we might use our *nous* and think on these examples for a little while longer.

APPLICATION: REFLECT

- We can be quick to adopt the notion of a Christian soldier fighting for his rights. We are less enthused, I suspect, about returning to the command post to hear our orders. Pray that God would tune your ears to hear His commands and soften your heart to obey them.
- Imagining yourself as a successful athlete for Christ is an attractive thought, yet Paul paints it to highlight the importance of remaining in the competition. Pray that you would not be distracted from your primary game plan of preaching and teaching the good news about Jesus.

- While growing up, most of us dream of being a farmer at some point. It seems a great life of outdoor fun. This is the superficial view, of course. Paul reminds us that the rewards are long in coming. The strength needed to continue with the long game is immense. Pray for that type of endurance in your walk with Christ, for the faith to endure and the presence of mind to push on in faith that the reward will come. Your efforts will be worthwhile on that day.

Instruments

Keep reminding God's people of these things. Warn them before God against quarreling about words; it is of no value, and only ruins those who listen. [15] Do your best to present yourself to God as one approved, a worker who does not need to be ashamed and who correctly handles the word of truth. [16] Avoid godless chatter, because those who indulge in it will become more and more ungodly. [17] Their teaching will spread like gangrene. Among them are Hymenaeus and Philetus, [18] who have departed from the truth. They say that the resurrection has already taken place, and they destroy the faith of some. [19] Nevertheless, God's solid foundation stands firm, sealed with this inscription: "The Lord knows those who are his," and, "Everyone who confesses the name of the Lord must turn away from wickedness."

[20] In a large house there are articles not only of gold and silver, but also of wood and clay; some are for special purposes and some for common use. [21] Those who cleanse themselves from the latter will be

instruments for special purposes, made holy, useful to the Master and prepared to do any good work.

[22] Flee the evil desires of youth and pursue righteousness, faith, love and peace, along with those who call on the Lord out of a pure heart. [23] Don't have anything to do with foolish and stupid arguments, because you know they produce quarrels. [24] And the Lord's servant must not be quarrelsome but must be kind to everyone, able to teach, not resentful. [25] Opponents must be gently instructed, in the hope that God will grant them repentance leading them to a knowledge of the truth, [26] and that they will come to their senses and escape from the trap of the devil, who has taken them captive to do his will.

Paul shifts from directly addressing Timothy and his faith to addressing how Timothy might further teach the Ephesians. Although this passage addresses corporate issues in the Ephesian church, the analogies are best understood on a personal or individual level.

Paul explains some of the issues Timothy must deal with in the church using generalizations about false teaching, quarrels, and gossip. He doesn't specifically identify what the false teaching was, which words were being dissected, or who was the subject of rumours. We might be tempted to extrapolate from the preceding chapter, but then we would find ourselves guilty of the very charges Paul instructed his disciple to avoid.

Instruments: 2 Timothy 2:14-26

He goes on to write about why such behaviours should be avoided. He uses an analogy about household utensils, using them to describe metaphors for gifts and talents and how some should be disposed of. The analogy only really works when we imagine it on an individual basis.

We all have giftings and skills, some of which gain attention and win praise from others, like the articles of silver and gold. Other skills and giftings aren't often seen, although they're still important to maintain our daily lives, like the articles of wood and clay.

We also have flaws which we exhibit when we use these tools for the wrong purpose or for dishonourable means. We might use our congeniality to manipulate or our serving heart to undermine others. Paul writes that if we are able to cleanse ourselves from these tendencies, we will be *"instruments for special purposes"* (2 Timothy 2:21). He then reiterates why we must rid ourselves of such tendencies and even tells us how we might do so.

The word instrument comes from the Greek *skeuos*, and it is more accurately translated as "vessel" or "container." It was used to describe a hollow object that could be filled. It was also used to describe people who could be filled with advice or instructions so as to represent their original instructor.

Paul therefore uses a play on words to carry his analogy from household utensils into a discussion of containers and subsequently into how one person can represent another, like a musical instrument being played by someone other than the original owner.

It follows that Christians are only useful instruments if they are emptied of their mouldy foodstuff and it is replaced with fresh produce. They can only be in tune with God if they play from His song sheet, not their own.

Understood on a personal level, we can apply the lesson more widely into a corporate setting, which perhaps was Paul's message to Timothy. There may have been some mouldy apples in the Ephesian church who needed refreshing.

The concept of being an empty vessel for Christ is worth revisiting as we think through applications of Paul's allegory in 2 Timothy 2:22–26. His picture is a reminder of the self-sacrifice, humble spirit, and self-effacement that is called for in the Christian life.

The self is to be emptied and the vessel is to be thoroughly clean—pursuit-clean (2 Timothy 2:22), pure-clean (2 Timothy 2:22), and not resentful-clean (2 Timothy 2:24). This is not to be a begrudging wash behind the ears to make ourselves presentable for a distant relative. We are to be thoroughly, enthusiastically cleaned, so that we are ready for noble purposes.

APPLICATION: INSTRUMENTS

- We use containers for many daily activities from packing lunch to storing leftovers. Next time you're cleaning a container, think on the importance of removing the prior contents and making sure it's ready for another use. Use this as a prompt to ask

God to clean your heart and make you ready for noble purposes.

- If we're going to be made pursuit-clean, experiencing no drag as we flee the evil desires of youth, then it will take a lot of soap, sponging, wax, and polish. Youthful desires don't go away, so this advice holds to all. Time and effort are needed for us to be made pursuit-clean. Take a moment to consider the things that hold you back from being the vessel God has called you to be. Let this lead you into prayer.

- Sometimes we serve in church but are resentful. This is not good service. It breeds bitterness. If this is your experience, speak prayerfully with those who organize church activities. It's better to be relieved from these duties than to be like mouldy produce.

No one sews a patch of unshrunk cloth on an old garment. Otherwise, the new piece will pull away from the old, making the tear worse. And no one pours new wine into old wineskins. Otherwise, the wine will burst the skins, and both the wine and the wineskins will be ruined. No, they pour new wine into new wineskins. (Mark 2:21–22)

Godliness

But mark this: There will be terrible times in the last days. ² People will be lovers of themselves, lovers of money, boastful, proud, abusive, disobedient to their parents, ungrateful, unholy, ³ without love, unforgiving, slanderous, without self-control, brutal, not lovers of the good, ⁴ treacherous, rash, conceited, lovers of pleasure rather than lovers of God—⁵ having a form of godliness but denying its power. Have nothing to do with such people.

⁶ They are the kind who worm their way into homes and gain control over gullible women, who are loaded down with sins and are swayed by all kinds of evil desires, ⁷ always learning but never able to come to a knowledge of the truth. ⁸ Just as Jannes and Jambres opposed Moses, so also these teachers oppose the truth. They are men of depraved minds, who, as far as the faith is concerned, are rejected. ⁹ But they will not get very far because, as in the case of those men, their folly will be clear to everyone.

Godliness: 2 Timothy 3:1-9

Imagine that you're seated in a restaurant and are handed a menu. As you read, you see that every dish has rainforest grubs, worms, or insects as its main ingredient. Whatever appetite you may have had when you entered the restaurant promptly disappears.

Looking over the list of vices in this passage will have a similar effect. Paul is describing the character of people in the last days. He uses the term "last days" loosely, in the same way it's used by other New Testament authors to describe the period of time between Jesus's first and second coming (Hebrews 1:1–2, 2 Peter 3:3).

It's tempting to believe that Paul is specifically addressing society in our time, since these ungodly attributes are sadly too familiar now. But I suspect many have thought the same over the centuries.

There is a natural transition in Paul's thoughts from 2 Timothy 3:5 to 2 Timothy 3:6–9. Commentors suggest that Paul, through the use of the idea of godliness, aligns these character traits with some members of the Ephesian church. Some of the false teachers fit this description, presenting a façade of kindness while holding hidden agendas.

The Greek word for godliness, *eusebeias*, is a composite word—from *eu*, meaning "well," and *sebomai*, meaning "to worship." This word might be used to describe authentic worship. It came to be used as an expression of dependency on the gods; in other words, it meant being humbled by our humanity. *Eusebeias* acknowledges that we are different from other animals and these differences have been bestowed by a divine source.

Exactly what is the difference between humans and other creatures? This proved difficult for the ancients to explain.

One difference is our yearning for spiritual enlightenment. As Christians, we point to the vision of eternity that's in our hearts. We highlight the *ruach Elohim*, the breath of God breathed into Adam (Genesis 1:27), or the manifestation of God's Son as a person. We speak of the appeal of God's ways to those who would listen, or the resonance we feel as Christians.

In 2 Timothy 3:5, Paul writes that some in the Ephesian church were outwardly human, having godlikeness, but failed to acknowledge the divine source of their humanity.

We might expect such ignorance from secular individuals, but it would have been unthinkable for Paul to expect this from one who purportedly believed in God. That would be a form of hypocrisy. Paul says that such people should be avoided. He declared them to have depraved minds.

Is there a chance that we don't acknowledge our godliness enough, that we don't reflect enough on our godlikeness?

If we don't acknowledge our divine origin, to whom are we giving worth-ship? If we deny the origin of what motivates us in church, are we not just worshiping ourselves?

In this potential deception, we see the importance of being the vessels Paul talked of in 2 Timothy 2. Only when we're cleaned and emptied can we be filled with the *ruach* of God. Only then can we be of any use for His purposes. Only then can we have genuine godliness.

APPLICATION: GODLINESS

- Appropriate godliness is to humbly thank God for His blessing to grant us the ability to live in a godlike manner. Our lot is not that of a nematode or mealy worm; it is to be human and live life in all its abundancy.

- Godlikeness has been bestowed on all humanity. In your interactions with others, take a moment to remember that we have all been created in the image of God. This is quite a thought and should alter our relationships.

- Our churches will be healthier than the church in Ephesus. Nevertheless, we would all benefit from showing a little more appreciation of the origin of our godliness. Pray for insight into the many ways we were created in God's image.

If I find in myself a desire which no experience in this world can satisfy, the most probable explanation is that I was made for another world… I must keep alive in myself the desire for my true country, which I shall not find till after death; I must never let it get snowed under or turned aside; I must make it the main object of life to press on to that other country and to help others to do the same.[19]

19 C.S. Lewis, *The C.S. Lewis Signature Classics* (New York, NY: Harper Collins, 2017), 114.

Convinced

2 TIMOTHY 3:10-17

You, however, know all about my teaching, my way of life, my purpose, faith, patience, love, endurance, [11] persecutions, sufferings—what kinds of things happened to me in Antioch, Iconium and Lystra, the persecutions I endured. Yet the Lord rescued me from all of them. [12] In fact, everyone who wants to live a godly life in Christ Jesus will be persecuted, [13] while evildoers and impostors will go from bad to worse, deceiving and being deceived. [14] But as for you, continue in what you have learned and have become convinced of, because you know those from whom you learned it, [15] and how from infancy you have known the Holy Scriptures, which are able to make you wise for salvation through faith in Christ Jesus. [16] All Scripture is God-breathed and is useful for teaching, rebuking, correcting and training in righteousness, [17] so that the servant of God may be thoroughly equipped for every good work.

The word convinced in 2 Timothy 3:14 is translated from the Greek *epistothes*, which was used to emphasize the assurance of a belief. *Epistothes* therefore more accurately refers to being *firmly* convinced or *firmly* believed. There is an additional level of reassurance that we might miss if we stick only to the New International Version translation.

We have admired this firm reassurance in Paul throughout 2 Timothy. We've been inspired by the apostle's dedication to Jesus despite his circumstances. We have reflected on the fact that this was in part a result of his dramatic conversion and understanding that the present was only temporary.

Gary Chapman, in his book *The Five Love Languages*, suggests that in marriage certain behaviours are more important than others to maintain the relationship. The love languages include gifts, acts of service, quality time, physical touch, and words of affirmation. He proposes that each person has one main love language. If our partner identifies our love language and communicates with us using it, we experience their love for us and are convinced that we're loved.[20]

This begs several questions: might we be convinced of Christ's love for us through the particular way His love is expressed? And if this is true, what was Paul's love language?

Paul's conversion was characterized by a physical interaction with the risen Christ on the road to Damascus. This was a defining moment for Paul in his relationship with Christ. It was the instant he became fully convinced of Christ's devotion toward him.

We might presume then that Paul's main love language was physical touch. For him, hugs and congratulatory handshakes or slaps on the back would have conveyed affirmation.

---

20 Gary Chapman, *The Five Love Languages: How to Express Heartfelt Commitment to Your Mate* (Chicago, IL: Northfield Publishing, 2010).

As we read of Paul's interactions with others, however, we don't see examples of this. What we do find is an emphasis on acts of service. Therefore, I suspect that Paul's primary love language was acts of service.

In our passage today, for example, Paul wrote of being rescued repeatedly by Christ. These rescues were as much spiritual as physical. This recurrence of service by Christ was important for Paul and convinced him of Jesus's ongoing love.

Very shortly, we will also read that he asks his son in the faith to perform a tremendous act of service and travel more than five thousand extra miles to bring him a cloak. This wasn't a test for Timothy; it's just what Paul had come to expect from someone who loved him.

In contrast, Timothy's love language seems to have been words of affirmation.

The letter of 2 Timothy is full of positive encouraging words from Paul. In today's reading, we see that he uses the word "you" seven times in seven verses to emphasize his affirming tone.

If words of affirmation spoke to Timothy's heart, we might also expect that these would be used by Jesus in his relationship with Timothy. We find this to be true in the current passage. Central to Timothy's conversion were the words of affirmation he found in the scriptures, whether these were taught to him by his mother and grandmother or expounded upon by Paul.

As Timothy's conversion came about through scripture, we should expect this love language to remain important to him as a source of Christ's love.

If Chapman's hypothesis about love languages is correct, then affirmation through scripture would have been important to keep Timothy afloat in his faith, just as acts of service were important to Paul.

In fact, we do find Paul encouraging Timothy to keep scripture central to his work and life. As scripture first appealed to Timothy, it apparently remained important as a way of continually appealing to him and convincing him of Christ's love. Being firmly convinced of Christ's devotion enabled Timothy to be more productive in his ministry as he led the Ephesian church.

Being able to recognize our own love language requires insight and contemplative thought. Knowing what made your heart tender towards Christ can help to keep it that way.

APPLICATION: CONVINCED

- Ask God to show you what it was about His Son that appealed to you and convinced you to become a Christian. See whether this fits with the love languages proposed by Gary Chapman: gifts, acts of service, physical touch, quality time, and words of affirmation.
- Reminding ourselves of what caused our conversion can be useful to offset any cooling off that may occur in the enthusiasm of our belief. Use the memory of your conversion to pray for a renewed conviction of the gospel.

- Words of affirmation from the scriptures helped to convince Timothy of Christ's love. The gospel story remains a powerful testimony. Thank God for His word and the reassurances and affirmation we gain from reading it.

The Word

2 TIMOTHY 4:1-5

In the presence of God and of Christ Jesus, who will judge the living and the dead, and in view of his appearing and his kingdom, I give you this charge: [2] Preach the word; be prepared in season and out of season; correct, rebuke and encourage—with great patience and careful instruction. [3] For the time will come when people will not put up with sound doctrine. Instead, to suit their own desires, they will gather around them a great number of teachers to say what their itching ears want to hear. [4] They will turn their ears away from the truth and turn aside to myths. [5] But you, keep your head in all situations, endure hardship, do the work of an evangelist, discharge all the duties of your ministry.

Paul used two strategies in his opening verses to 2 Timothy 4 to rouse Timothy from any languor that might have set in from reading this long letter.

He charges Timothy, commanding him, and in doing so draws him to attention. Paul then uses a peculiar phrase to refer to spreading or declaring the gospel: "Preach the word." This phrase is overfamiliar to us, but it wouldn't have been stale to first-century readers. In fact, it would have captured their attention.

It's likely that Paul wanted to provoke Timothy, so he used an unusual slogan to reawaken him to the importance of both scripture and the gospel.

The word preach, in the Greek, was *kerusso*, which describes news being delivered from a governor or other dignitary. It implies enthusiasm and forthright declaration, like a trumpet blast. Timothy was not to simply talk about the word; he was to eagerly, wholeheartedly speak it with clarity and purpose.

Paul used *logos* for "the word." He didn't use the word for scriptures, nor did he use the one for gospel or Christ or the message of salvation. He deliberately used *logos*. Paul's choice reminds me of the beginning of John's Gospel, which was probably completed between AD 64–70, around the time Paul wrote this letter.

Paul, like John, uses this phrase to identify Jesus. Jesus is the reason, the logic, the founder of order and purpose, the creator. Using *logos*, both Paul and John neatly wrap all these thoughts into a single maxim.

Using this phrase to describe Christ has a dramatic and poignant effect, both on Timothy and on modern readers.

Paul had several motives in writing 2 Timothy, one of which was to encourage Timothy in the pastoral duties he performed in Ephesus, since he had encountered false teaching. Paul compelled Timothy to stick with the gospel and not detract from its teachings.

False teaching can be deliberate. Sometimes clear falsehoods are proclaimed with the goal of personal gain. False teaching can also be the result of distracted teaching.

"Preach the word" is a rallying cry against both types of falsehoods, but in its rousing terminology it is particularly useful as a reminder against distracted teaching. Distraction can readily lead to us missing important issues, or missing important falsehoods, that can spoil our perception of the gospel.

Psychologists would tell us of two forms of distraction: inattentional blindness and change blindness.

Inattentional blindness is seen most days in people using their cell phones and walking into objects. Inattentional deafness is also common; this is seen when people miss important auditory stimuli like bicycle bells or car horns while listening to music with their wireless earbuds.

From the pulpit, inattentional teaching can occur when our focus is distracted by polemic arguments, perhaps ones related to identity or church policies. When falsehoods are missed, false doctrines spread.

"Preach the word," Paul encourages. In doing so, he prods us awake so that we may avoid inattentional distraction.

Change blindness is a different type of sensory distraction. From the pulpit, this might occur when people are overfamiliar with a particular message, so much so that they fail to spot the introduction of a subtle flaw. Like a red dot appearing in the periphery of a familiar painting, we might miss it. A visitor will readily notice the same flaw, though.

Unless our almost hypnotic state is aroused, we'll be oblivious to the blot on the landscape, the error in the exposition.

"Preach the word," Paul reminds Timothy, urging him to guard against change blindness. He compels Timothy to see the truth—speaking, proclaiming, and focusing on Christ.

We shouldn't let our overfamiliarity with this message lead to informality or laxity. Paul intended Timothy to sit up and take notice; his choice of words was to sound to Timothy like out-of-tune bagpipes or a clanging gong or crashing symbol.

APPLICATION: THE WORD

- Take a moment to reflect on the beginning of John's gospel. *Logos* encapsulates the divine essence of Christ with inspirational originality. Pause and consider all that John tells us of Jesus in John 1:1–5.
- Even in prison, even at the end of his life, Paul entreated Timothy not to lose faith, not to lose hope or lose sight of Christ. He might well have written, "Do not be blinded by circumstance or surroundings, for these are distractions." Pray for Paul-like commitment to the truth in your telling of the gospel.
- Take stock of your own inattentional misperceptions. These might be experienced while on the phone or listening through earbuds. Use the insight you glean in these moments to thank God for Christ.

The Word: 2 Timothy 4:1-5

In the beginning was the Word, and the Word was with God, and the Word was God. He was with God in the beginning. Through him all things were made; without him nothing was made that has been made. In him was life, and that life was the light of all mankind. The light shines in the darkness, and the darkness has not overcome it. (John 1:1–5)

Crown of Righteousness

2 TIMOTHY 4:6–8

For I am already being poured out like a drink offering, and the time for my departure is near. [7] I have fought the good fight, I have finished the race, I have kept the faith. [8] Now there is in store for me the crown of righteousness, which the Lord, the righteous Judge, will award to me on that day—and not only to me, but also to all who have longed for his appearing.

In writing about suffering and end-of-life matters, Paul raises two issues that could undermine Timothy's faith, or our own. Death and suffering are difficult topics and ones we tend to avoid. Our lack of engagement can be a source of weakness in our faith. The absence of depth in our understanding means that when we face suffering or end-of-life matters, we become less certain of our foundations.

In these three verses, Paul considers his sacrificial life and impending end. He is emboldened by their spectre rather than weakened, reassured rather than dispirited. He continues to look to Christ as a righteous judge to award his salvation.

He wrote in 2 Timothy 4:6, *"For I am already being poured out like a drink offering, and the time for my departure is near."*

This verse, like Philippians 2:17, speaks to how Paul saw his life—as a gift to others. He envisaged the drink offering that was poured out on the altar in the Old Testament period. That same drink offering was poured onto other sacrifices, whether grain or animal, and served as a forerunner of Christ's blood. It's also representative of the wine at the last supper.

The drink offering is a useful metaphor of life not ebbing out of a Christian like a retreating tide, but rather being poured out deliberately as they give themselves up in the service of others.

Paul knew his resources were running low, that if his life was a portion of wine then it was almost spent. In this he demonstrates insight into his situation.

His attitude was not one of a headless fool walking straight into danger. Paul was not in denial about the precarious nature of his predicament. He was not in a hypnotic state or psychosis. Paul knew the likely course of events and was reminded daily of the fragility of his physical existence. Yet he remained resolute in his faith.

Paul was a model of stalwart service, and his example is challenging to emulate. We tend to avoid suffering, not fully embracing it as a part of our Christian lives. We avoid talking about it and try hard not to experience it.

Our reluctance to consider suffering comes from fear and denial. The fear is understandable, as no one should enjoy suffering. It is not inappropriate. We must manage our fear, for our path is not to be uncertain; we are not to be paralyzed, like a deer in a car's headlights, nor are we to always look to the fight, like the lion.

To manage our fear, we need to overcome our denial and accept that suffering, like death, is inevitable. Once we accept that suffering is inevitable, the challenge becomes how to persevere and endure in the face of suffering.

Our question isn't whether we will suffer, but how we will manage the suffering. Will we be able to bear the circumstances as Christ and Paul did?

If suffering is inevitable, our view should be like the child looking towards adulthood, acknowledging it and understanding that responsibility, leadership, and hard work will soon be theirs.

Through this analogy, I am reminded of the four pillars that define Christian adulthood: rejecting passivity, taking responsibility, acting courageously, and expecting a greater reward.[21]

These same four pillars are found in Paul's example of Christian service. The soldier doesn't just turn up to the battle with passive acceptance; he rejects passivity and fights the good fight, taking responsibility for his role. The athlete doesn't just compete but has the courage to see the race to its conclusion. The farmer always works for the greater reward; he doesn't seek to feel satisfied with his day's work but instead labours to provide a greater crop.

Will Timothy be able to mirror Paul's approach to service and suffering? Will he be able to say, like Paul, that he has been poured out willingly and intentionally, like a drink offering?

21 Robert Lewis, *Raising a Modern-Day Knight* (Carol Stream, IL: Tyndale House, 2007), 60–61.

Will we? I hope so, but I sense that knowing how to approach suffering will help enormously during times of difficulty. It is helpful to consider Paul's examples of the soldier, athlete, and farmer, just as it is helpful to consider the four pillars of adulthood. The last of these, expecting a greater reward, links suffering with the other potential source of uncertainty: eternal life.

Life after death is one of the biggest theological blind spots of our modern churches. It simply isn't scientific enough for our postmodern world to talk of life after death. When it's raised as a potential reality, we become too unsure and uncomfortable to discuss the issue. We then find no solace, for we feel no certainty in our reward.

In response, Paul wrote of the crown of righteousness that was in store for him in heaven (2 Timothy 4:8). The crown he spoke of was not a kingly crown, a *diadem*, but rather a *stephanos* crown, a winner's wreath. This was the prize he so coveted that he was able to suppress his fear of the future.

The *stephanos* crown was awarded to athletes in games or other competitions. It was usually a humble crown, but receiving it was a reward unto itself. The reward was not in its precious material but in the preciousness of the works that led to it being awarded.

Paul maintained his focus in the heat of suffering by concentrating on the expectation of his greater reward. Receiving the winner's wreath was the acknowledgement he sought from Christ, an acknowledgement that his life, which had been redeemed, had been lived well, in obedience, and in a manner pleasing to the Father and the Son.

I think Timothy desired the same for himself. Recognizing this, Paul encouraged him to pursue Christianity, to pursue it despite the possibility of suffering and sacrifice.

A question we face, just like Timothy, is whether we can thrive in the life that leads to the crown. Like a child who looks toward adulthood, we don't know what trials lie ahead. A child has the examples of his parents, though, and the ideals of the four pillars of Christian adulthood, the most important of which is the last: the expectation of a greater reward.

The essence of the reward is what keeps the farmer ploughing on. It's what motivated Paul. If we are to find courage, take responsibility, and reject a passive life, we, like Paul, Timothy, and Christ, will need to desire a *stephanos* crown.

APPLICATION: CROWN OF RIGHTEOUSNESS

- Think for a moment of your own approach to suffering and death. These unpleasant topics are inevitable consequences of the fall. Pray for the courage to approach any fear or misgiving you may have toward these topics and find the strength to ask Jesus for His companionship throughout life, including the unpleasant aspects.
- Consider the four pillars of Christian adulthood. These are useful guidelines to be reminded of when life is difficult. Pray that you would be mindful of them in testing times.

Crown of Righteousness: 2 Timothy 4:6-8

- A crown of righteousness is in store for those who persevere in their faith. Paul paints this picture to encourage strength and endurance during trials. Pray that Paul's metaphor would be a source of encouragement for you as you walk with Jesus in uncertain times.

Stand By

Do your best to come to me quickly, [10] for Demas, because he loved this world, has deserted me and has gone to Thessalonica. Crescens has gone to Galatia, and Titus to Dalmatia. [11] Only Luke is with me. Get Mark and bring him with you, because he is helpful to me in my ministry. [12] I sent Tychicus to Ephesus. [13] When you come, bring the cloak that I left with Carpus at Troas, and my scrolls, especially the parchments.

[14] Alexander the metalworker did me a great deal of harm. The Lord will repay him for what he has done. [15] You too should be on your guard against him, because he strongly opposed our message.

[16] At my first defense, no one came to my support, but everyone deserted me. May it not be held against them. [17] But the Lord stood at my side and gave me strength, so that through me the message might be fully proclaimed and all the Gentiles might hear it. And I was delivered from the lion's mouth. [18] The Lord will rescue me from every evil attack and will bring me safely to his heavenly kingdom. To him be glory for ever and ever. Amen.

Stand By: 2 Timothy 4:9-21

[19] Greet Priscilla and Aquila and the household of Onesiphorus. [20] Erastus stayed in Corinth, and I left Trophimus sick in Miletus. [21] Do your best to get here before winter. Eubulus greets you, and so do Pudens, Linus, Claudia and all the brothers and sisters.

Paul's second letter to Timothy is often portrayed as a piece of personal correspondence meant to affirm. We have touched on this, highlighting how Paul, with his concrete, unmovable faith, sought to reassure and solidify Timothy's belief.

When we consider our own faith, I suspect we feel more often like Timothy than Paul. We carry a degree of uncertainty with us that needs a course correction. We too benefit from reading Paul's words of affirmation.

In our uncertainty, we can feel weak and unworthy to be in Paul's company. It's reassuring to read in today's verses that Paul also felt moments of weakness. At times, he required the presence of a stronger force to pull him back on course (2 Timothy 4:17).

As a result of the desertions, Paul was left feeling isolated. In his isolation, he missed the strength of fellowship. He felt the absence of coworkers. Alone, his frailty was apparent and on display during his trial. He felt weakened by his loneliness, separated from others and under pressure to conform, to give in and stay quiet about his faith.

Paul was honest to Timothy about these feelings, and his comments are likely to have affected Timothy emotionally. Here was the solid, dependable Paul, admitting that he had moments of weakness. Paul confessed to having some of the same tendencies

127

he had noticed in Timothy. I'm sure Timothy was refreshed to encounter his teacher's humanity.

Reading these verses may also have tugged at Timothy's heart, for he would have readily empathized with Paul in his weakness, reflecting on his mentor's desperation in confessing such feelings.

In response to his weakness, Paul wrote that the Lord strengthened him. The Greek word for strengthen is *endunamoo*. This is a composite word, from *en*, meaning "in," and *dunamis*, which is translated as "power." When Paul appeared in front of the court, he felt empowered and energized. Although he was at a low ebb in his own resistance, he felt Jesus beside him.

The expression "stood" comes from *pareste*, which speaks to being beside or alongside something. The term conveys authority or responsibility being given over to something next to it.

Imagine a working horse that struggles to pull a heavy cart. Once another horse is harnessed alongside it, responsibility is given over to the new horse to manage the load.

Paul felt a surge of relief and was strengthened. In sensing the resurrected Christ's presence next to him, the miraculous presence of the risen Jesus, Paul felt empowered. In his weakness, he felt strong.

What greater lesson could Paul leave with his disciple than to confess to similar feelings as those he saw in Timothy and explain how those feelings could be resolved in a real and personal way?

Paul's experience before the Roman officials would have been harrowing. He was singled out to take responsibility for his life, actions, and beliefs. Paul was called to give an account of himself. In those moments, he realized his frailty, failings, and weakness.

This provides us with a picture of the final judgment, including images of the reckoning we will experience before God. Our moment before the Father is an inevitability we cannot avoid. Let us pray that, like Paul, we can call on Jesus to stand by our side and empower our salvation.

APPLICATION: STAND BY

- It is reassuring to observe moments of fallibility in our heroes of the faith. These weaknesses are not character deficiencies but opportunities for us to rely on Christ, like Paul did. Thank God for Paul's honesty and pray for the insight to call on Jesus when you need Him to stand by.
- Think of what it looks like to coming alongside another. This is a helpful picture of how Christ strengthens us. He pulls us through our trials like a partnering horse. Thank Him for His empowerment.
- It is a sobering thought that someday we will stand before God and give an account of ourselves. We won't be alone, though, and we have no reason to be afraid, for Christ will stand alongside to make the case for our salvation. Take a moment to rejoice in this and let this realization lead you to thank Jesus for His life.

Your Spirit

The Lord be with your spirit. Grace be with you.

Paul's benediction to Timothy is a personal one. The your in *"your spirit"* is singular. And although the sentiment is similar to the closing of Galatians and Philemon, this signoff is more pointed.

Pneumatis is the Greek word translated here as spirit. It was used to describe moving air, in the same way that *ruach* was used in Hebrew. *Ruach* was distinguished from *ar*, a different word that was used for air that didn't move. It's also distinct from *shamaiyim*, used to refer to the sky or atmosphere. Similar distinctions were used in Greek, with *aer* being used to describe unmoving air and *aether* referring to for atmosphere, or thin air.

Pneumatis came to represent the presence of life, since breathing symbolized the difference between the living and the dead. *Pneumatis* was the lifeforce. When present, it was associated with being alive; when absent, a person had passed away, their spirit/breath no longer present. The body thus became inanimate or lifeless.

Pneumatis was also used to describe the divine power of God's essence. The expression *theo pneumatis*, or God-breathed, was used to describe the divine inspiration of scripture in 2 Timothy 3:16. It is the breath of God that imparts spirituality, or God's image, to humanity (Job 32:8, 33:4, John 3:5–8).

At the beginning of this letter, Paul wrote of seeing Timothy's spirit once Timothy had received the Holy Spirit (2 Timothy 1:7). Paul returned to this theme, reaffirming Timothy's spirit with encouragement and reassurance. He ended with a personal affirmation.

Paul, perhaps drawing on his own experiences of Christ standing by him to empower his witness, prayed that the Lord would be with Timothy's spirit.

Paul knew that Christ alone, through the Holy Spirit, would enable the lessons he had given to Timothy to have an impact. Paul was passing along responsibility to Christ for Timothy's spirit/life.

The expression *"the Lord be with your spirit"* is not a resignation of responsibility. It was written with joy. Paul was acknowledging the role of the Lord of all creation, the Lord of all things who grants, restores, and perpetuates life. Into His almighty power Paul was delighted to hand over Timothy's future.

Timothy's salvation and sanctification was never Paul's sole responsibility, but as his father in the faith Paul felt a natural duty born of fatherly love.

Here in the last recorded written words of Paul we see a beautiful picture. At the end of this personal letter, at the conclusion of his teaching, we read his last shouts of affirmation. In them, we encounter a reminder from Paul to his disciple that

Timothy's spirit was with Christ. Paul's prayer was that it would remain there—strong, self-disciplined, and unafraid.

APPLICATION: YOUR SPIRIT

- There is no more readily accessible application than to use our breathing as a reminder of our faith.
- Take a long, deep breath. As you exhale, feel blessed that you, like Timothy, are in the hands of your Creator.
- Take a long, deep breath. As you exhale, pray for a sense of the peace Paul felt in handing over Timothy into the care of Jesus.
- Take a long, deep breath. As you exhale, say a prayer of thanks for the apostle Paul and his ministry.

Reflections

2 TIMOTHY

You then, my son, be strong in the grace that is in Christ Jesus. (2 Timothy 2:1)

2 Timothy was the last known writing of Paul. In this letter, Paul seemed to be aware that his time was running out. He was aware that this imprisonment might be his last. Death seemed imminent. In that context, the letter has an air of a last will and testament.

In light of such sentiments, at times I've found it difficult to put to one side the sadness of the context and find uplifting messages. Rousing verses are present though and like many others, I have heard inspiring sermons on passages from 2 Timothy. 2 Timothy 1:7 is frequently quoted, as is 2 Timothy 4:2. There are others. The familiarity of these verses speaks to the popularity of 2 Timothy and its usefulness to emphasize salient messages for those who work to spread the gospel.

It is also possible that some have heard sermon series on the whole book of 2 Timothy. I have been blessed to have listened to excellent expositions by gifted preachers, and these messages have returned to me as I reread the letter. I remember lessons to pursue courage and preach the word.

Whether it's in a sermon series or from selected passages, 2 Timothy has an appeal to modern readers. Part of the appeal is that the book speaks to all mentors, and we all, whether we recognize it or not, are mentoring someone. 2 Timothy is a note from a mentor to his mentee. As mentors to others, or as mentees of others, there are perspectives and peculiarities here that we can learn from, but to do this we need to put aside our sadness at saying goodbye to Paul.

As a reflection on Paul's perspective, I was struck by his opening statement in 2 Timothy 1:1 declaring his identity. Given the pressure on him to accept other views of himself, this was sobering. It reminded me that I am first and foremost a disciple of Jesus.

Considering some of the points he makes to Timothy, I was encouraged by the reminder that reassurance can come from scripture. At times I have looked for more solid manifestations of God for reassurance. These are present when I think back at prior blessings, but sometimes in the moment, in the present, I hope for something more tangible.

It was extremely helpful therefore, to be given a reminder from Paul that the Bible and the gospel can be a solid affirmation of the genuine nature of our faith. It's also helpful to hear that scripture was an important source of personal inspiration for Timothy, both in his journey to conversion and in his continued pilgrimage in his faith.

Some peculiarities in the letter made me smile. These aren't inconsistencies but quirky comments that portray the humanity in Paul and emphasize the depth of his relationship with Timothy.

No peculiarity is quirkier than the request for his cloak. The request was reasonable enough, until you consider the distances involved! There was a direct sea route from Ephesus to Rome that Timothy could have taken. However, retrieving the cloak in Troas would have necessitated an 8,500-kilometre trip, one way. This was no ordinary request.

Other peculiarities can be seen in the metaphor of the farmer to visualize a faithful Christian, as well as in the reference to itchy ears in 2 Timothy 4:3. Both analogies work. Agrarian communities would have readily understood how faithful a farmer must be in order to prosper. "Itching ears" may have been a secular term used to describe how people sought out entertaining speakers.

Even though these terms fit their context well, Paul's personality is expressed in their usage. He used his experience of different cultures and participation in temple discussions to create vivid images that emphasize his teaching points.

Aside from the perspectives and peculiarities of 2 Timothy, an underlying theme of the letter was Paul's gratitude for Timothy. He was thankful to Timothy for his companionship, and thankful to God for providing such a devoted disciple.

I think this latter point is my greatest lesson from the letter, a reminder that God presents opportunities like Timothy to us during our lives. Acquaintances, neighbours, friends, or even family members are all potential Timothys. May we pray more readily and more frequently over those we meet so we don't miss the opportunities God presents us with.

Not everyone we meet will retrieve our comforting cloak, but perhaps a handful of people in our lifetimes will consent to share a pilgrimage long enough for us to truly appreciate them as Paul did Timothy.

For Further Reading

Walter L Liefeld, 1&2 Timothy/ Titus: NIV Application Commentary (Grand Rapids, MI Zondervan, 1998)

William Barclay, The letters to Timothy, Titus and Philemon: The New Daily Study Bible (Louisville, KY: Westminster John Knox Press, 2003)

D. Martyn Lloyd-Jones, I am not ashamed: advice to Timothy (Grand Rapids MI, Baker House Publishing 1992)

The Greek translations in this book have been paraphrased from material found at: "Verse by Verse Commentary by Book," *Precept Austin*. Date of access: August 16, 2023 (www.preceptaustin.org/verse_by_verse).

Proceeds from the sales of this book will be donated to St. Timothy's Christian Classical Academy, Ottawa.

ST. TIMOTHY'S CHRISTIAN CLASSICAL ACADEMY, OTTAWA

St. Timothy's is a small interdenominational Christian school with students from Senior Kindergarten to Grade Eight. It was founded by a group of Christian families in 2005. It is a charitable organization and seeks to offer classical education in a Christian environment to children from a broad range of backgrounds. This is achieved through generous provision of tuition assistance.

The dedicated faculty at St Timothy's seeks to lead their students to revere truth, desire goodness, and rejoice in beauty. The school has been housed in several locations throughout Ottawa since its inception but would ideally seek to establish a home for itself.

In the meantime, the school continues to be a beacon for Christ in the inner city. St. Timothy's strives to bless children, parents, and the broader community so as to fulfill the ambassadorial role that Paul strove for in his pupil Timothy.

Further details can be found online: www.st-timothys.ca

LOCAL CHURCH, OTTAWA

Gary Small and his family attend LOCAL Church, Ottawa, which was established in 2018. It is twinned with its sister campus in Tauranga Moana in New Zealand.

The church preaches and professes a Christ-focused message. It has generous ministries in local and international charitable giving. LOCAL promotes the benefits of small group discipleship ministry.

More details of the ministry and work of the church can be found online: www.localchurch.co

A WORD FROM HIS WORD
BY GARY R. SMALL

Each chapter of *A Word from His Word* focuses on a single word or phrase from a short biblical passage. It is the author's prayer that by returning to a simplified but effective approach to Bible reading, your daily times with God's word will be invigorated. Enjoy the entire series!

NOW AVAILABLE:

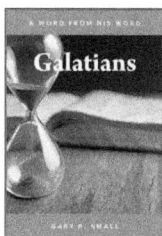

Galatians	*Colossians*
Ephesians	*1&2 Thessalonians*
Philipians	*Philemon & Titus*

COMING SOON:

Romans

1 Corinthians

2 Corinthians

www.ingramcontent.com/pod-product-compliance
Lightning Source LLC
LaVergne TN
LVHW051411080426
835508LV00022B/3031